Rusty

A Dog and His Angels

Cindy Devereaux

BALBOA.
PRESS

A DIVISION OF HAY HOUSE

Balboa Press books may be ordered through booksellers or by contacting:

Balboa Press
A Division of Hay House
1663 Liberty Drive
Bloomington, IN 47403
www.balboapress.com
1-(877) 407-4847

Because of the dynamic nature of the Internet, any web addresses or links contained in this book may have changed since publication and may no longer be valid. The views expressed in this work are solely those of the author and do not necessarily reflect the views of the publisher, and the publisher hereby disclaims any responsibility for them.

The author of this book does not dispense medical advice or prescribe the use of any technique as a form of treatment for physical, emotional, or medical problems without the advice of a physician, either directly or indirectly. The intent of the author is only to offer information of a general nature to help you in your quest for emotional and spiritual well-being. In the event you use any of the information in this book for yourself, which is your constitutional right, the author and the publisher assume no responsibility for your actions.

Any people depicted in stock imagery provided by Thinkstock are models, and such images are being used for illustrative purposes only.
Certain stock imagery © Thinkstock.

ISBN: 978-1-4525-7449-3 (sc)
ISBN: 978-1-4525-7451-6 (hc)
ISBN: 978-1-4525-7450-9 (e)

Library of Congress Control Number: 2013908829

Printed in the United States of America.

Balboa Press rev. date: 9/16/2013

For
Jean Elizabeth Thompson

Introduction

Before Rusty entered my life, I had the pleasure of owning three other dogs. All of them were affectionate, intelligent and wonderful pets. The same can be said of Rusty with one additional fact: he became one of my greatest spiritual teachers.

This terrier-chow-angel mix of a dog taught me lessons in trust, unconditional love, surrender and forgiveness.

We shared many adventures; I rescued him three times -- two of which are recounted in the following story. For his part, he sometimes rescued me from loneliness, boredom and sadness. I can honestly say that my faith was greatly strengthened because of this magical and amazing dog's presence in my life.

He brought me many moments of pure joy.

Together we experienced God's grace, His loving protection -- and the presence of angels.

For this I will always be grateful.

- Cindy Devereaux

For reasons of privacy, some individual's names have been changed --but every word in this story is true.

Chapter 1

"Until one has loved an animal, a part of one's soul remains unawakened." -- Anatole France

This story is about a very special part of my spiritual journey, and how I walked it accompanied by a beautiful and loveable dog named Rusty.

It all began when I was living with my Dad, Alexander Boynton, in Brooklyn, N.Y.

One day I returned home from New York City and was surprised to find a cute and friendly dog in the yard. He had been given to Dad by my niece Chantal and her mother because they were about to move into an apartment complex that had a 'no pets allowed' policy. Dad said that a woman who lived across the street was going to take him -- after she had a fence built.

Twelve joyful years later, Rusty was still with us.

This loving, funny, magical and playful dog earned nicknames like "My Sweet Puppito," "My Hunk of Burnin' Furry Love" (thanks Elvis), "The Puppy Dog Love of My Life" and my favorite: "God's Puppy." I used to say his name was "Rustipher Pierre – Rusty, for short."

He loved to cuddle. He would also walk up to me and simply lean against my leg. One of his favorite love moves was to walk over to you while you were seated and walk one way while rubbing against your legs, then turn around and walk back the other way - repeating this gesture. I soon decided that this was his way of giving me hugs.

There is a driveway between Dad's house and the next door neighbor's. At the front of it is a locked gate. The side door on our house faces the side door of theirs. Dad didn't see any reason to keep this door locked during the daytime. Rusty would simply let himself out and scratch on the door when he wanted to come back inside.

He had an energetic fan club of little children. Every day, on their way home from school, they would loudly call his name. Then he would let himself out and run to the gate to greet them. They all seemed to be talking to him at once, as they pet him through the gate.

This was a daily routine.

All of the neighbors adored him. One of them volunteered to walk him and another would bring him food. Dad, of course, kept him well fed with dog food as well as food from the dinner table.

Even after one of the neighbors moved away, he would come back to visit his family and still take time to walk Rusty.

I loved to take him for long walks. When we got home he would try to stay out longer by swinging me around so that we could walk some more. Many times, during these walks, people would say that he looked like a lion. Many times he did - especially when the hair around his neck grew long and actually looked like a lion's mane.

At night Rusty would sleep in the bedroom with me. When I went away, he would sleep in Dad's room. I'm a professional singer and sometimes I'd go on extended tours out of the country. Whether I was returning from the airport or from the local subway, I would always look for Rusty at the front gate before entering the house. We'd say our hellos through the gate and then I would go into the house while he barked loudly until I let him in -- then there would be doggie kisses and yes, Rusty style hugs.

He had such a joyful nature and especially seemed to love playing and spending time with boys of all ages. One day I saw him on his hind legs and he appeared to be boxing with my brother Sean. Yes, it was definitely a boy thing! That was for the boys; cuddles were for the girls.

Dad had retired many years before Rusty's arrival, so the two of them were able to spend a lot of time together. My stepmother passed away many years earlier; since this is a two family home and the neighbors on the block adored him, Dad was never alone.

There was always a recliner in the front parlor. When one wore out, a replacement was quickly found. Dad would sit on it, either watching television or reading a newspaper with Rusty lying beside him. They started out the day watching "The Price is Right" and ended it watching "Wheel of Fortune." When Dad went outside, so did Rusty. When Dad walked to the front of the driveway, so did his sidekick.

I especially cherish two pictures I took of them. In the first one they're standing at the front gate looking out at the street while Dad is locking the gate for the night. Then I took the second picture after the two of them turned around and walked, side by side, back down the driveway. Dad may have only taken three minutes to do this but Rusty was still going to accompany him. For me, those two pictures always sum up Rusty's relationship with Dad.

One of Rusty's best friends was my nephew, Gerald. He visited from California a few times a year. When he first arrived at the house, Rusty would jump up and down loudly barking. Gerald once said "he reminds me of a kid." I felt that way too. It was as if he were my little brother or my child. When I came home with packages, he would jump up on the sofa and poke his nose through them to see if there was anything for him. At those times, the "like a kid" opinion really made sense.

Chapter 2

"Animals share with us the privilege of
having a soul."-- Pythagoras

One day my brother Justin came by and said something that I never expected to hear anyone say. Referring to Rusty, he said "I don't like him." At the time, he was sitting in a chair adjacent to the sofa. Rusty climbed up on the sofa and looked directly at him, as if to ask: "Can you look me in the eyes and say that?" Dad and I both laughed. At the time, I dismissed that comment as the rest of us had deep, everlasting love for Rusty and having the nickname God's Puppy does come with certain obvious privileges. Besides how could the entire neighborhood, passing strangers and the rest of the family be wrong?

Now Sylvester was a different story. Sylvester was an orange colored cat owned by the next door neighbors. He was also a frequent visitor -- climbing into the window box, and looking inside the house. Dad sometimes left cat food outside for him. Once in a while Rusty would see Sylvester at the window and let him know, in no uncertain terms, that he was not welcome. One day I saw Sylvester give Rusty a look that I thought cats could only do in cartoons. His face was so contorted with anger, that he actually looked dangerous. Fortunately the window between them was safely closed.

Sylvester knew that.

He was a very bold and wise cat. Sometimes he would enter the house and walk around. I guess he must have checked to see if Rusty was outside before making such a courageous move. Those two not liking each other somehow made sense. Why a human could say he didn't like Rusty, I will never know.

One year, I decided to spend my vacation in Paris. When I hear the song "J'ai Deux Amours, Mon Paix et Paris" ("I have two loves, my country and Paris") – I always think that it was written especially for me because that is exactly how I feel about my country and that beautiful city.

I could easily walk the length of Paris and still be ready to walk some more.

One afternoon, while leaving the section surrounding the beautiful and opulent Opéra Garnier, I decided to walk down Avenue de l'Opéra -- and to my surprise -- found Brentano's, an American bookstore. Since I love browsing and shopping in bookstores, I quickly walked through the door.

I found the metaphysical section and my eyes rested upon a book called *The Four Agreements* by don Miguel Ruiz. I opened a page at random and started reading a story about a woman who came home from work one night feeling emotionally tense, tired and headachy. Her little daughter, who she adored, was singing loudly. Because of the state she was in, the mother only wanted peace and quiet and the singing made her headache worse. She became angry and told her child to be quiet because her voice was "ugly." The little girl grew up thinking her voice was displeasing and hearing it --would only disturb others. Because of these thoughts, she never sang again.

I thought "I've got to read further and check this author out" because when I was young, I was criticized, by relatives, for wanting to sing professionally. One of them told me over and over that I couldn't sing -- even though she had never actually heard me.

I didn't listen.

It had taken classes with many spiritual teachers, reading scores of metaphysical books and a move to Paris, to get those voices out of my head. I learned how to allow myself to freely follow my dreams. Now I found someone who was writing about a little girl who stopped singing because she agreed with her mother's assessment of her voice. don Miguel explained that we have to be mindful about the agreements we make with ourselves. They can actually change our lives.

I was definitely going to read this book.

I returned to New York and began having dreams about a brown skinned man with wavy black hair. He didn't speak or move around so I had no idea what his presence in my dreams meant. He simply appeared briefly, leaving me wondering who he was.

Soon after, I received a catalogue from The Omega Institute in Rhinebeck, NY and it advertised a five day retreat with don Miguel Ruiz teaching *The Four Agreements*.

This was the name of the book that I found in Paris.

I looked at don Miguel's picture and also realized that he was the man I had dreamt about. Plans were quickly made to attend this retreat.

I did, and it was a life changing experience.

As part of the retreat, don Miguel taught us a shamanic ritual called the "Mitote Ceremony" where we forgive, release and detach from all the hurts and dramas we are carrying around. Some of the descriptive words for mitote are: confusion, disturbance and commotion. These are negative situations in your mind that need to be removed and replaced with peace.

Before the ceremony, you find a stone. You choose a notebook and begin by writing a description of the stone as if it were your body. Then you write a heading at the top of another page that says: "This is my last judgment." After signing your name and dating it, you write a title that says: "The Judge." Under it you write your story. This will include any negativity that is taking up space in your mind and robbing you of your peace. When this is complete you write another title called "The Victim." Under this heading you write out the question: "How did this make you feel?" To respond, you list all of your emotional reactions to the experiences you are judging. It ends with a sacred ceremony where you kneel and with one hand you hold the stone up to the sun (Father Sun) for "blessing" and with the other you are touching the earth (Mother Earth) for "nourishment." Then you stand up and all of these issues that you wrote about are blown into the stone seven times.

After that, you bury the stone.

I found this to be very effective because it either erases the negative situations from my memory or if I ever think about them again, it is totally without any emotional attachment. It feels as if I've surrendered the drama – and reclaimed my peace of mind.

I was doing a mitote ceremony, by a garden, at the end of our driveway. I decided to do the "burial" part of the ceremony there.

While I was finishing, Rusty walked down the driveway. Instead of running up to me as he usually did, he sat a respectable distance away as if he understood that a sacred act was taking place and he was to sit there quietly. At one point it looked, and felt, as if he was totally in touch with what I was doing. It made me feel wonderful. He was calm and poised and there was a radiance about him. With the sun shining down on him, I thought "he looks majestic." I don't know why I was surprised. Many times my sweet dog did the right thing at the right time.

Chapter 3

"Who can believe there is no soul behind those luminous eyes?" – Theophile Gautier

Like most dogs, Rusty was terrified of thunderstorms. He would climb up on the bed and cling to the mattress, as if his life depended on it.

When he first came to live with us, he was afraid to go downstairs to the basement. This fear lasted until one day there was a thunderstorm and all the humans were -- in the basement. He quickly made the decision that joining us there was safer than staying upstairs with all of that horrific noise.

After that storm, the basement became one of his favorite hangouts.

One evening we were walking around the corner from the house when suddenly a car came to a screeching halt. It narrowly missed hitting a toy poodle. The owner ran out into the street and picked up her dog. Seeing that the little dog was safe, we continued our walk.

We walked for several blocks and then turned around and headed back towards the house. All of a sudden I heard someone yelling. I looked across the street and there was the same woman holding the little dog in her arms. She was saying: "wait." Of course we did. She crossed the street, stooped down and placed her dog's face near Rusty's. Then she said: "you almost got killed trying to see him – so there he is!"

She introduced her dog as Bijou and explained that every time she walked past Dad's house, her dog would pull her in the direction of the gate so that she could see Rusty. Seeing him outside of the gate got her so excited that she threw caution to the winds and risked her life to be near him.

Rusty's fans were not just humans.

Another evening, I was on the phone trying to reach a customer service representative at one of my credit card companies – a rather frustrating task.

I was given one prompt after another. If it's this: press one, for that: press two. "Calls will be answered in the order received. Please stay on the line, a representative will be with you shortly." I was getting more and more frustrated and tired of holding the phone. All I wanted was a human voice to take my call and answer a simple question. I must have been on hold for at least fifteen minutes!

Suddenly Rusty walked in, joyfully wagging his tail, stepping on the phone wire and disconnecting the call! After two seconds of shock, all I could do was laugh and hug him.

He was so cute.

Chapter 4

"My little dog – a heartbeat at my feet." – Edith Wharton

One New Year's Eve Dad, Chantal, Rusty and I had a little celebration at the house. All of us, including Rusty, were wearing party hats. He had his water while we drank sparkling apple cider. We took lots of pictures and joyfully welcomed in the New Year.

It was one of the best New Year's Eve parties I have ever attended!

I once teased my niece about how they had given him away and how lucky we were to have kept him. She defensively replied: "I had nothing to do with it -- I was eight years old at the time!"

This information was helpful because, for the first time, I had an idea of Rusty's possible age.

I came home from church one Sunday and the gate was unlatched and opened. Rusty was at the far end of the driveway. Something had happened to his back leg and he couldn't walk on it. I carried him up the stairs. A neighbor came over and wrapped the leg. Then I called a few veterinarians. Since it was Sunday, I was getting one voice mail after another. Finally I got someone who said they were closed but could see him the next day, without an appointment, "if it's an emergency." I somehow had the feeling that he had been hit by a car.

It was just a feeling.

I had an appointment in New York City the next day but naturally decided that Rusty's wellbeing would be my priority; if he wasn't better by the next morning, I would take him to the vet's office.

The next morning he was still limping and I was in tears. I cancelled my appointment and got ready to take him to the doctor. A young man, who was working for my father, came over to accompany us. I asked him to carry Rusty in his arms. I thought getting him off of his feet would lessen the pain and also emphasize the emergency aspect of the visit.

When it was our turn, the vet's assistant placed Rusty on the examining table; he removed a few ticks and asked me if I wanted an x-ray done. I said "yes." As Rusty lay on his back waiting for the x-ray. I told him not to be afraid -- to remember that he was "God's Puppy." The veterinarian gave me a look as if to say: "finally, somebody gets it."

The x-ray showed that the bone in his injured leg was not connected to the spinal column. I was told that this could be the result of being hit by a car or it could be congenital. I was given a renewable prescription and told to keep him in a small area so he couldn't do too much walking. He was given a rabies shot and a license. The doctor said that Rusty was a terrier-chow mix. He added that my estimate of his age was most likely correct because, in his words, "he still has that puppy energy."

While we were waiting for the prescription and the bill, Rusty walked around the waiting room and greeted every single dog. They all acknowledged him – except one. This was a Scottish terrier who was sitting on its owner's knee. Not to be ignored, Rusty stood on his hind legs and placed his front paws on the owner's other knee. It looked as if he'd decided to speak nose to nose with this pretty little dog.

Yes, this was the same dog that had to be carried in and now he's standing up on the knee of a stranger just to say hello to another dog.

He didn't seem to care about his injured back leg. Being friendly was more important.

Chapter 5

"The world is a book, and those who do not travel read only a page." --Saint Augustine

One of my favorite times of the year is Christmas in New York City. I love the energy, the decorations and simply put -- the holiday spirit. But there was one Christmas when I felt the need to escape from the city. It was Christmas 2001. We had all been shocked and saddened by the events of September 11th and there was no way I could feel the usual holiday spirit after what had been done to my city. Yes, like millions of others, I took that event personally.

My friend Arne invited me and my best friend Howard Richmond to spend the holidays at his home in Stockholm, Sweden and we accepted.

Stockholm was beautiful and snowy. While I wasn't used to darkness falling at around 2:30 in the afternoon, it was lovely. I felt as if we were living inside of a Christmas card.

We ended up staying for a month.

One day I realized that Rusty's prescription would need to be refilled and I would have to make arrangements to have someone pick it up. I could not think of the name of the vet. I called home and no one there could remember it either. I finally went online and found his phone number. I called his office and paid for the refill over the phone with my credit card. The vet's office called Dad and my brother Sean picked it up so that my 'sweet puppito' did not miss a day.

One day, after returning home, I was petting Rusty and noticed that the name and phone number of the vet were imprinted on one of the tags attached to his collar! Oh well, if he could have talked, I'm sure he would have shared this information with us - after he stopped laughing!

Chapter 6

*"Our perfect companions never have
more than four feet."* -- Colette

Dad's house is a large, two family home. The second floor was occupied by his long term tenants. His section of the house has two bedrooms with one more in the basement. The basement has a large recreational space, a laundry area, two storage closets and a bathroom. I decided to sleep in the basement. Rusty, as usual, followed me.

In the summer I opened a door in the bedroom that led to the garage. Houses built in a certain period had garages built inside of them. The car was always parked on the street so the air in the garage was clean. Rusty sometimes chose to leave the bedroom and sleep on the garage floor. I guess he enjoyed the coolness of the cement.

I loved the idea that he was comfortable and nearby.

Dad was not alone upstairs; he had a tenant using the other bedroom. He was a family friend named Alan. During the week, he drove a school bus. One Sunday he decided to sleep in. Rusty missed seeing him so he went to the door and started barking.

I know that animals have instincts that sometimes save lives, so I decided that I'd better check this out right away. I knocked on the door and Alan sleepily answered. I apologized for the intrusion and explained that Rusty was barking at the door because he hadn't seen him all day and was worried. He expressed his gratitude for our concern and after Rusty was assured of his safety, he went back into the bedroom.

This dog was full of surprises. I thought: "any day now, I expect him to form full sentences." One day, as I was leaving, I went to the gate and said "take care of Dad." He made two grunting sounds causing me to wonder: "Did he just say okay?"

Once in a while, when we were walking around the neighborhood, I would hear a little child say: "that looks like Rusty." When I replied: "it is," they would express joy at seeing him outside of the gate. I'd hear this same remark from adults with sterner voices. After telling them who my father was, they would smile and calm down. This is a neighborhood where people care about each other and they didn't want to think that some stranger was walking away with Dad's beloved dog.

Chapter 7

"Animals are such agreeable friends – they ask no questions, they pass no criticisms." – George Elliott

I moved to Orange County in upstate New York. Since it was two hours away from Brooklyn, I still spent a lot of time visiting Dad and Rusty. On each visit Rusty and I took our long walks around the neighborhood and Dad and I watched movies, went shopping and had lots of fun. Sometimes Dad put me to work. I would sort out his bills, write out checks for him to sign, or help him find missing items.

One night, my brother Justin called. He said that he was at the ASPCA trying to claim Rusty.

Dad had gone to bed the night before and had forgotten to bring him inside. There had been a thunderstorm and, in a panic, Rusty had broken through the gate and run away. The next morning Dad discovered an open gate and a missing dog.

Dad was devastated. My brothers and the neighbors searched all over the neighborhood. Flyers were made and distributed. Finally my brothers checked with the ASPCA.

Fortunately, Rusty was there.

The veterinarian's phone number was found on Rusty's collar. When the shelter called, they were told that the records listed me as his legal owner. This meant that I was the only one who could claim him.

I spoke to someone at the shelter and assured them that I would be there the next day to bring him home.

I was very upset and frightened. I had heard stories about wires getting crossed and animals being erroneously euthanized. I thought about how frightened he must have been and quickly made plans for the trip. I also began sending mental messages to him. I kept saying over and over "don't worry I'm coming. I'll be there."

That felt like the longest bus ride I have ever taken. After arriving in New York City, there was a subway and another bus to take in order to get to the house. Dad, of course, was sad and I fought to contain my anger. Our friend Mr. Wilson drove me over to the shelter and with Dad's one hundred dollars for shots, a microchip and a new license -- we were ready to bring our dog home.

When we arrived, we were shown his picture in the computer. I identified him. Then they said that we'd have to wait awhile as some of the shots are not administered until the owners show up to claim their pets. While we were waiting, we asked where he had been found. The receptionist showed us the report. Mr. Wilson read it and said that he had to have crossed Kings Highway in order to have been captured at that location. A busy highway at night! I was just happy that my amazing dog was safe and hadn't been hit by a car or mistaken for a lion! We were even able to laugh when we read that Rusty's name was listed on the form as "Bruno."

A young attendant came out and said "I'm glad someone came to pick him up. He looked so sad. I must have given him seventeen dog biscuits!" Finally, my hunk of burnin' furry love (thanks again Elvis) was brought out. He was happy to see us. Mr. Wilson took the leash from the attendant. As we walked to the car, Rusty held us up by trying to sniff every inch of the floor -- and the parking lot.

When Rusty got home he stayed near Dad for a little while, then we went outside. A little girl came by and was happy and surprised to see him. She ran down the street shouting "Rusty's back." She quickly returned with two other children. As they pet him through the gate, one of them asked: "Rusty, where did you go?"

I finally calmed down and got ready to leave. After descending the steps, I looked back and saw Dad and Rusty standing in the doorway side by side. Dad had this big, beautiful smile on his face and Rusty was radiating his usual adorable and loving energy.

It was a scene that I will never forget.

On the way down the street, I met my brother Sean. In a subdued voice, and looking towards the house, he asked: "is he in there?" I said "yes" and he said my other brother had wondered if I was going to show up at all. He said his response had been "of course – it's for Rusty."

Mr. Wilson told me that Rusty had given them a very bad time for about two weeks after his return home. Looking back I'm not surprised since he'd been locked up and given rabies shots, antibiotics, a medicine to prevent kennel cough, and a tracking microchip. I can only guess that his erratic behavior might have been a combination of side effects and fear.

The thing that I will always be grateful for is that he was found, kept safe and returned to us.

Chapter 8

"Make yourself familiar with the angels, and behold them frequently in spirit, for without being seen, they are present with you." -- Saint Francis of Assisi

There were many special and sometimes magical moments with Rusty. One example, strange as it seems, would be the day that I felt so ill and weak that I literally crawled up the four steps that led from the side door into the kitchen; Rusty walked over to me and lovingly licked my face. Another time was when I overheard my niece Chantal asking my father why Rusty spent so much time with me when I visited. Dad's reply was: "because she hugs him."

I didn't think anyone noticed.

I had been reading many books by Doreen Virtue on angels. When I was asked to list my favorite books on a social media site, I listed a few titles and added: "anything by Doreen Virtue." I was also purchasing her CDs and cards as well as listening to her online every Wednesday on Hay House Radio. She calls her program: Angel Therapy ®.

Doreen had prayed for ways to help bring peace to the world following the September 11, 2001 tragedy. She was guided to create a day where people around the world could connect with God and the angels in prayers for world peace. The event was named "International Angel Day" and scheduled for September 10, 2006. Workshops were to be presented all over the world and ten percent of the entrance fees were to be donated to children's charities.

I decided to attend a gathering in New York City, facilitated by Angel Therapy Practitioner ® Berry Milton Jones, III.

We did angel card readings for each other, had discussions about the angels, prayed and danced. One of the students returned after the lunch break and showed Berry a white feather that she'd found in the doorway.

White feathers are often described as "calling cards of the angels" – one of their ways of letting us know that they are near.

One of our exercises was to ask Archangel Michael to give us a message in response to our questions. Archangel Michael's name means "he who is like God" and he oversees lightworkers.

We were to ask a question, get still and write down the answers that we were given.

My question was about my music career. I listened for answers and wrote a few paragraphs. I expected it to be all about music and career concerns-- but it was not. One sentence said: "don't worry about Rusty – the angels are looking after him." I thought it was a nice idea but I had no idea why this would be necessary. Rusty was home with Dad doing all kinds of fun things. His friends, young and old, were greeting him at the gate and visiting him in the house. He was well fed, happy and healthy.

I learned in *A Course in Miracles* that I cannot judge. One of the reasons it gives --for not judging -- is that we don't know the past, present and future of any situation. I read that sentence about Rusty without having an emotional reaction. In retrospect, I can see that Archangel Michael was telling me not to worry about Rusty because he and the other angels knew what was waiting for him in the future.

I did not.

While I was at the workshop, two of my sisters had come from Virginia to visit Dad. At the time, I did not know that this visit was because he was not feeling well. Even though I spoke to him every week and visited him often, he had not shared this information with me.

He was still driving, shopping, hanging out with the neighbors and smoking two packs of cigarettes a day.

Chapter 9

"The soul is here for its own joy. The only lasting beauty is the beauty of the heart."--Rumi

The apartment upstairs became available and my brother Justin and his youngest daughter Olivia moved in; they were soon joined by his girlfriend Cara and her daughter Brianna. Neighbors and friends were running in and out of the house to visit my ailing father. Some came to converse and pray with him. Others brought him plates of food.

At first, I visited only on the weekends and eventually stayed longer. I accompanied him to some of his doctor's appointments; sometimes we shopped together – and other times, he gave me a list and sent me to the stores alone.

Dad had lung cancer.

My sisters and nephew Gerald came to visit him. Dad also had the assistance of home health care attendants. Hospital equipment was moved into his bedroom and a "no smoking" sign was posted on the front door since there was an oxygen tank in the house.

He had what is called: in-home hospice care.

His friend Cornelius came over every day to visit and find out if he could be of service in any way. Dad was beginning to spend a lot more time in bed. One day I was standing in the hallway and watched as Rusty walked into the bedroom. Dad was fast asleep. Rusty raised his head to look at him; he seemed to be scanning Dad's body as he looked and moved his head from side to side while sniffing loudly -- then he left the room.

I thought it was beautiful watching him check up on his best friend.

Dad was hospitalized twice. The second time, when I went to bring him home, the doctor asked me to leave the room. Dad said "no – she can stay." Then the words "we cannot do anything more for you" were spoken. Dad showed no visible reaction to this news and I was in a strangely non-reactive state as well. I saw no reason to discuss this with anyone as everyone knew what was to come.

Dad was in the care of daytime home health care attendants and there was a head nurse who checked in with him once a week. Soon it was determined that he had reached the stage where the services of an overnight attendant were needed.

I had gone back home and when I returned I met the overnight nurse. She immediately told me how much she loved Rusty and added: "he looks like a lion." The head nurse was on the phone. She looked at me and explained to the party, on the other end of the line, that Dad was now getting someone overnight because my brother Justin was feeling "overwhelmed and stressed out."

This was not the truth.

My brother said that he had taken off from work for the weekend because Dad's condition had worsened. I concluded that it sounded as if things were "shutting down." He agreed.

The following Monday morning, a new health care attendant by the name of Michael arrived. He showed me a letter of recommendation from a family, that he had previously worked for, and quickly began to look after Dad. I told him that my sister Dolores' married name was the same as his last name and that she was flying in from California the following Wednesday. He said that he was looking forward to meeting her.

Justin and Mr. Wilson were busy doing some repairs on the side door.

Around three o'clock, Michael came into the kitchen and said "Miss Cynthia, we have a problem." I went into the bedroom and he said: "he has no pulse." I ran to the phone and shouted to my brother and Mr. Wilson "Dad has no pulse." They ran up the stairs to the bedroom. Dad's friend Cornelius also raced there --as did Rusty.

Rusty then lay down by the head of the bed. There was no other place for him to be.

As instructed, I called the head nurse and she arrived quickly. She examined him and announced "no heartbeat, no pulse."

Dad was gone.

A few hours later, the funeral parlor attendants arrived to take him away. I told my brother that I would have to leave the room as I couldn't bear the thought of watching Dad leave his beloved home – or me.

I went down to the basement. I don't know what Rusty did. I do know that I watched him go into that empty bedroom the next morning, crying as he circled the room. Later on I was told that he was seen walking and sniffing around the recliner – as if he expected to find Dad there.

Chapter 10

"We should remember in our dealings with animals that they are a sacred trust for us from our Heavenly Father."-- Harriet Beecher Stowe

After Dad's memorial service, I watched as my brother Justin and his girlfriend quickly began to take over the house. One of their first rules was that Rusty could no longer come into the dining room, the living room or the parlor. I was beginning to think that he was being treated like Heathcliff in *Wuthering Heights*. In that story, Heathcliff had been found and adopted by the kind and generous master of the household. After his death, the son told Heathcliff that he was no longer welcome in the house and would have to live outside, in a shack – as a servant.

I was not too far from wrong.

A wooden child safety gate was placed in the doorway leading from the kitchen to the other rooms; I overheard my sister Florence tell Cara, that Rusty had urinated in the living room

– but not to worry, she would ask her friend Joe if he knew anyone who wanted a dog.

As far as I knew, he was emotionally upset and that was no big deal. This is a dog that had lived peacefully all over the house for twelve years. He had the occasional "accident." We just cleaned it up and life went on. After all if that happened over night – how could he be expected to go outside? The side door was, of course, locked at night and everyone was asleep.

On at least two occasions (early in the morning), Rusty had licked my hand to wake me up and let me know that he needed to go outside. He had other signals too and they worked perfectly when members of the household were awake.

My sister Jean had come up from Virginia to help care for Dad. During that time, she and Rusty had become very close. One day when I was visiting, he entered the room and started whimpering loudly. She said "alright, Rusty" -- raced to the side door and let him out. Apparently, the two of them had set up a signal – one that said "I need to go. Will you please let me out?"

Now there were strangers deciding his future. As a lawyer would say "I rest my case."

One afternoon, I was sitting in the parlor watching a movie with my sisters Jean and Florence. Rusty, no longer allowed in the parlor, was way back in the kitchen (behind the wooden gate) – crying.

He couldn't understand why he wasn't allowed to sit with us – as he was used to doing. The crying was non-stop. Jean got upset. She said "I can't take this -- I'll still hear him crying like that, when I get home!"

I finally couldn't take it anymore either and left the room to watch the movie in the back bedroom – with him. My sisters came to the back of the house too. I heard Florence say to him "are you satisfied? You made everybody come back here."

No, Rusty was not the one who did that.

My brother had a female Rottweiler named Sunshine. She was kept in a cage. Since his daughter, Olivia, had allergies I thought, perhaps, that was the reason for caging the dog. Later on I was told that she wasn't allergic to dogs.

The reason for doing that remained their secret.

Later on Sunshine was put in the unoccupied bedroom in the basement. The cage went with her, but the door was open, so she was free to walk around the room.

Sunshine was beautiful and friendly. During my visits, I would play with her and clean her up with dry shampoo for dogs. It was understood that any food that I bought for Rusty was to be shared with Sunshine.

One time she physically got in my way to keep me from leaving the room. She clearly did not want to be left alone. While I truly loved spending time with her – I had to leave - and quite frankly getting out of there that day was a little bit scary.

Chapter 11

"A righteous man cares for the needs of his animals......." Proverbs 12:10 NIV

Before ending my extended stay in Brooklyn, I decided to buy as much dog food as I could load into a shopping cart. Candy, containing arthritis medication, was purchased for Rusty. Then I made the decision to schedule my visits so that the food I bought could last from one visit to the next. Logically, the people living in the house would be expected to provide food for the dogs; I just thought I should help.

The truth is: doing this made me feel good.

My brother, his girlfriend and two children were living in the second floor apartment of the house. No one was sleeping downstairs. This disturbed me because it meant that Rusty was alone overnight. Later on Cara's son moved in and was given a bedroom on the first floor. Rusty was able to sleep next to the boy until there was the "problem" of dog hair getting on the boy's clothing. Rather than move the clothes, Rusty was barred from the bedroom.

Dad had purchased a cordless pet vacuum. It vacuumed excess hair, to prevent shedding, and also functioned as a hair brush. I used it and left it in a closet. The next time I visited, it was missing. I looked all over the house and finally found it in the basement. It was damaged and useless. When I mentioned this to Cara, I was given a cold reaction that clearly said "so what!"

Now Rusty was being left alone, no one cared about grooming him and he was no longer allowed in the little boy's bedroom – because he was shedding hair – after one of them had removed and broken his grooming device.

There was no longer a bowl of water left on the kitchen floor for him. The bowl outside was filled with dirty water. A neighbor told me that the children kept adding clean water to it -- without first emptying out the dirty water and cleaning the bowl.

Later on Rusty would be diagnosed as being "severely dehydrated."

I wanted to bring him upstate to live with me but my lease had a "no pets" clause. It also said if you needed to have an animal, for emotional support, and got a letter from a doctor or a psychiatrist then that clause could be waived. My brother said that he knew a psychiatrist who could help, but my sister Florence advised me that this would not be a good idea. Her reason was that we live in the age of computers and that kind of information could one day be used against me. While I would have loved to have had the attitude of "I don't care" – I was living with a roommate who said "no" to the idea as well.

Sunshine was being left in the backyard. One day when I went there to see her, she got up on her hind legs and put her paws on both my shoulders. I really felt as if I was being hugged; she was happy to see me and I was deeply moved by the greeting.

During one of my visits, it began to rain and I went inside to ask Cara if I could bring Sunshine inside. She said she would have to call my brother at work and ask him. She did. He said "no."

His dog was left outside in the rain.

Both dogs were being left outside during the day. Sunshine was often tied up and Rusty was free to roam all over the driveway and the backyard. Sunshine was in heat. Rusty, being a male dog, behaved in a predictable manner. This eventually led to her attacking him.

I noticed that Rusty was losing a lot of weight; I had been told that Sunshine had gotten much thinner too. My brother and his girlfriend talked about Rusty's weight loss as though it were a joke. They actually laughed about it.

My friend Pauline told me that the whole neighborhood was talking about how Rusty was being treated. I continued to visit with his food and arthritis candy. We took our long walks and there was lots of the usual petting, cuddling and hugging. I made sure that I carried a brush to groom him. As a precaution, I took it home with me to make sure that it wouldn't disappear or get damaged.

On one of my visits, my brother said that they had given Rusty some new food and that he'd gotten diarrhea all over the back of the house. This was followed by a new rule. He would no longer be allowed inside -- under any circumstances.

I did some research and found out that any sudden change in a dog's diet, living circumstances or emotions can lead to this type of illness. My precious dog was suffering from all three symptoms.

It seemed as if they were punishing him, once more, for something that they had done.

A neighbor told me that she had witnessed Rusty's distress at being left outside during a thunderstorm.

Besides cleaning and feeding Rusty, I had given myself the 'job' of cleaning the driveway. The dogs had defecated and it looked as if no one had cleaned the area for at least two weeks. Dad had either done this job himself or someone who was working for him had taken care of it.

Sunshine was not only thin -- she had flies nesting all over her back. I could not walk her but I could give her food and water. One time when I poured water into her empty bowl, she jumped up on her hind legs in order to drink it in mid-air!

The front gate had a latch on it and remembering how Rusty once pushed his way through it, I decided to reinforce it by wrapping two luggage bungee cords around it. One day I noticed that they had been removed. I asked no questions. Later on, my sister Florence told me that Rusty had chewed through them and run away. The children had looked for him and a little boy from the neighborhood found him and brought him back.

No one living there thought I needed to be told about this.

The last time that I went to the house, I was greeted by Cara's children. The little girl saw the food that I was carrying and said "I'm glad you're here, there hasn't been any dog food in the house for a few days." The little boy added that he was happy that I had the arthritis candy -- "because he really needs it." That could only mean that Rusty was limping and no one bothered to call me to ask what to do or if I could bring something to help him.

Dad had a very tall fig tree in the backyard. Every year it brought forth so many figs that he had enough to spare and to share. I felt that there was something special and otherworldly about owning a fruit bearing tree. I always saw an abundance of figs on the branches as well as on the ground. They were juicy and delicious. Dad would happily share them with me, his friends and the neighbors. Even after giving them away, there were many leftover.

This year something different was being done. The bottom branches of the tree had been taped to the trunk. When I asked what the purpose of doing this was, I got a very strange and surprising answer.

"We did this so that Rusty couldn't eat the figs."

By now, Rusty had lost so much weight that I could practically see and feel his ribs. He was emaciated. Most of the pigment on his nose had turned pink. He had what is sometimes called 'winter nose' – a condition that can be caused by sickness, trauma or cold weather.

He was certainly traumatized and the nights were getting colder and colder.

I sat outside with him and he leaned against me. There could be no tight hugs or even a bath -- because he was simply too fragile.

At one point I went inside and Brianna, rolling her eyes, said: "you're not bringing him inside, are you?"

I knew that I had to do something. I felt that if I didn't – my sweet dog would be dead in two weeks.

When it was time to say goodbye, I called him to the gate as I always did. At first, he didn't want to come to me. I could feel him asking me "how can you leave me here, like this -- with these people?" I had to make a quick choice. Something had to be done. I could not allow this to be done to this sweet, beautiful animal.

By now, the only reason for my visits was to see Rusty and bring him food.

A few days later I went to a pet supermarket, purchased a large quantity of premium dog food, called United Parcel Service and shipped it to Brooklyn.

I wouldn't be able to see him but I would know that he was being fed.

Chapter 12

"Watch with me angels, watch with me today." -- A Course in Miracles

The first thing that I was guided to do was to call Doreen Virtue on her online radio show. She is a spiritual clairvoyant and her program is called Angel Therapy ®.

I had been reading her books and using her cards for several years with great results. She gives readings during the show and I desperately needed to know what to do about Rusty, so I decided to call her.

First, I called on Lord Ganesh ("the overcomer of obstacles") to help get me on the air.

It was September 10, 2008. The true significance of this date will be explained later. There was some kind of temporary on-air glitch and then I heard Doreen's theme music and a voice asking me what my question would be. I said it was about my dog. I was told that this would be a suitable question for the show, if I were chosen, for a reading.

The show began. There was what I can best describe as a booming sound. Then it was announced that there was some sort of "technical difficulty."

Finally, Doreen began:

Doreen: Well I made it! I didn't think I was going to be with you live for awhile with some sort of technical difficulty –but we're here...yes...prayers do work and I want to thank Steve and everyone else in the Hay House radio booth for their tenacity in getting me on the air today. Thank you guys!

She proceeded to talk about how much she enjoyed International Angel Day in San Francisco and introduced a new set of cards called "Angel Therapy Oracle Cards." She then pulled a card (Heart Chakra) and read its meaning out of the accompanying guidebook. The reading was followed by a talk and a beautiful meditation.

Then the phone call-in segment of the show began with Doreen saying: "so lets talk to the angels and get some loving messages--and where do you want me to go angels?"

Doreen: OK, they want me to go to line 7 and speak to Cindy. Hi Cindy, you're our first caller today. How are you?

Me: I'm great. How are you?

Doreen: Good, good. How can we help you?

Me: My concern is with my dog, Rusty. My Dad passed away a few months ago and the dog was in his house and my brother has moved in with his girlfriend and some children and they were supposed to be looking after my dog. The dog has lost a lot of weight. When I visit from upstate I always buy food and bring him arthritis medicine but I thought it was just like a gesture...and then when I go back...I've gone back twice....he's lost more weight. One of the children told me last week, he hadn't had any dog food in a few days. So I've tried to get in touch with an organization that, you know, is a shelter because I can't bring him to my apartment.

Doreen: Right.

Me: And I'm waiting to hear. It's a shelter that keeps the animals alive and I told them I would volunteer, donate, you know perform at their functions – do anything if they could take him. I haven't heard yet and I know you can tune into him. I want to know how he feels about it cause they're keeping him outside 24/7; he's used to being indoors. He's about 13 years old and I'm very stressed and sad about it.

Doreen: I know baby. I want to ask you something cause I'm getting a strong hit that there's a listener - Cindy, I'm not going to tell where she is, but she's on the east coast. Upper east coast – tri-state area. That there's someone listening who would take Rusty and give him a very good home. But we'd need to give out some sort of contact for you – either an email address or website if you'd be willing to do that.

Me: Of course I would.

Doreen: OK let's give out something where someone could contact you about Rusty. Alright?

Me: Ok. Umm – oh dear.

Doreen: And if you don't feel comfortable, I can ask you to email it to Betsy in our office and then people could email Betsy.

Me: OK. It's Cindy. C.i.n.d.y. @cindydevereaux.com.

Doreen: Betsy, if you get that too: Cindy@cindy devereaux.com and you can always email Betsy at betsy@ angeltherapy.com to get the email address. Rusty definitely has a broken heart over your father and is off his food -- as well as the actions of your brother and the children. So it's playing together there. I do see your dad watching over you very, very strongly and oh and that's your brother; ok I was going to say do you have a brother and you just told me you did –and your brother... and the angels keep showing me someone with a motorcycle. You know who that is?

Me: There's another brother who has borrowed people's motorcycles but I don't know if it would be him.

Doreen: It felt like a brother who was using a motorcycle and just to let you know that he's being watched over and is safe --I thought it was the brother that had moved in but it makes sense it's the other brother. Your father's showing me that he's very busy watching over the family and that there's a young girl also. Is that your daughter?

Me: No

Doreen: There's a girl, there's a young girl. He keeps pointing to a young girl. She's not very old at all. This might be with the brother.

Me: There's a little girl who moved in with my brother's girlfriend and I think she's an Indigo and she's the one who told me that the dog hadn't had food in a few days.

Doreen: Oh, that's what it was. That's what it was. Yes.

Me: It might have been her. She's like a little fairy.

Doreen: Yes, it makes sense. She's adorable. She's beautiful.

Me: I'm working with one of your Angel Therapy Practitioners, by the way.

Doreen: Oh, wonderful.

Me: In New York and.....

Doreen: Good, good. We have wonderful angel therapy practitioners all over and they're listed on angeltherapy. com. Let me just see since we're going into the break in just a minute...what else is going on here. Well the dog, they're showing me has some sort of allergies or something with the skin and it's like something's irritating the skin and that's also making him not want to eat as much. I don't feel like he's not being fed – it's like he doesn't want to eat because he's emotionally very upset right now and there's a need for him to be washed. There's something on his skin that's irritating him. I don't know if you're washing him. I don't think its fleas

– it's almost like some kind of powder or dust or something. There's an allergen.

Me: There's a scratch on him the last time I saw him and he's lost so much weight I couldn't hug him and I couldn't even brush his hair.

Doreen: I'm going to ask everyone who's listening to pray for Rusty and for the whole family of course -- and we ask that the listener who knows that they are the one to go help and rescue Rusty that they get in touch with you right away. I want to thank you so much for calling Cindy and know that our prayers are with you and I'm so glad you're our first caller today. You're obviously an Earth Angel who's very compassionate and please, take a deep breath.

Me: (Audible breath)

Doreen: And all these feelings, share them with God and the Angels. Don't try to do this alone. OK? Cause you're definitely not alone.

I later emailed Jillian Miller, my Angel Therapy Practitioner®, to tell her about my conversation with Doreen. She wrote back: "this matter will be concluded very swiftly."

She was right.

Chapter 13

"Now faith is the substance of things hoped for, the evidence of things not seen."-- Hebrews 11:1 (KJV)

The next day I received guidance to call my friend Marilyn Martin. We met when we were neighbors in an apartment building in Soho (New York City). I remembered that she had told me that one of the other tenants was rescuing animals. I called to find out if she could possibly help Rusty and was told that this woman was only finding homes for cats. She then suggested I call her cousin Tonya Martin, who is an animal rights activist with many connections. I took the number and quickly made the call.

Tonya was very gracious and willing to help. She said her friends owned a pet shelter and gave me their phone number. I called them right away and was told that they were renovating and wouldn't be able to admit any new animals for a few months.

Then a shelter in New York City was suggested. I called and their voicemail message said that they are a "no kill" facility, but if overcrowding becomes an issue, they might be forced to reconsider this policy. That didn't feel right, so I dismissed it as a possibility.

Tonya said that she and a neighbor were making a few calls and that it would be easier to place him if I provided a photo. I found a very cute one. Although it was taken when he was younger, I felt that with his weight loss – it would be suitable.

I was about to find out how generous and wonderful people can be.

Tonya emailed his picture to her contacts in the animal right's world and many of them subsequently forwarded it to their contacts.

The following is one of Tonya's first emails:

NYC OWNER DIED DOG LIVING OUTSIDE URGENT HE IS A "SENIOR": Under this headline, were these words: "A friend's father passed away and his dog Rusty is now in the care of her brother who is not caring for him or feeding him regularly. He was exclusively an inside dog when her father was living but is now living outside 24/7 and has lost a lot of weight due to depression and irregular feedings. My friend has sent over a supply of food so that he will now be fed regularly.

I am trying to find him foster care or a permanent home, I would take him in but I took in a rescue cat which sent my older cat to the hospital - a dog in the house would surely push her over the edge. The no-kill shelter I work with isn't taking in new dogs at the moment and I'm not sure where else to go.

Here's what I know: he's a 12 year old male terrier/chow mix, very friendly, seems to be in good health, likes the neighborhood children and is currently living in east Flatbush. My friend is willing to pay for a full vet checkup and help subsidize foster care if necessary. Photograph of Rusty is attached; please let me know if anyone is interested in adoption or fostering Rusty.

This email had over 50 addressees and they were asked to forward it to their individual lists.

At the very beginning of the search, one woman offered money -- another toys and a trip to a pet adoption fair. We received copies of emails that were cross posted. A woman suggested a shelter that only takes dogs whose owners have passed away. It's located in Avon, NY and a death certificate must be provided.

His picture was placed on petfinder.com.

Another person wrote "this poor guy is not looking or feeling so good since his owner passed on. Is there anyone who could help him?" Then she offered to help out financially should he get adopted or placed in foster care. She ended her email with "please cross post far and wide for exposure. This poor guy should be helped, not a good situation. He is in a not so good state. Thank you......!!!!! He is a cutie, he really is....."

By now I was feeling zoned out. I knew what I had to do, but I felt as if I were doing it on automatic. It was a strange kind of detachment; as if I knew it was all going to work out and my role was that of an observer. Maybe that was protecting my emotions or maybe that's what happens when you call on angels for assistance and they take over.

My niece Chantal called me for some advice about an upcoming audition. During the call, I told her that I was going to have to give Rusty away. I could tell by the sound of her voice that this news upset her. She and her mother were not able to keep him when they moved, but she visited her grandfather often, so she (still) got to spend a lot of time with Rusty.

I called an upstate New York shelter. I thought that if he could stay there, I would still be able to visit him. I would volunteer there as well. My phone call was sent straight to voicemail and my email got no response. My sister Dolores said that if I could work it out with them, she would help by sending money to pay for Rusty's transportation from Brooklyn. I thought that I would ask one of Dad's friends to drive him to the shelter. I couldn't forget that one of them had told me that Rusty's condition was "the talk of the neighborhood."

No one was happy seeing him losing weight and being forced to live outdoors.

Chapter 14

"If you have men who will exclude any of God's creatures from the shelter of compassion and pity, you will have men who will deal likewise with their fellowmen." -- Saint Francis of Assisi

I had decided to go to a gym to check out the possibility of taking yoga classes. Afterwards I went across the street to a restaurant for a quick snack. As I was leaving the restaurant, my cell phone rang. It was Howard. He said that Tonya called and left a message that she needed to speak with me, as soon as possible, because she was going to go to Dad's house to pick up Rusty. I was in a large parking lot and it was cold and noisy so I raced into a store and asked permission to use my cell phone. I told them that it was about "rescuing a dog" and with their permission, I made the call.

Tonya said that her friend had read about Rusty and demanded that she pick him up immediately as the forecast was for an extremely cold night and the idea of him spending it outside was not acceptable.

I called Cara and told her that Tonya was coming over to pick up Rusty. I explained that he was going to the vet the next day, and asked her to send some food along with him. She agreed to get him ready and wanted to know when to expect Tonya. When I called Tonya, she said that she was "practically in front of the house."

Tonya's next call was that she'd picked him up and was taking him to her home. Later on she told me that he was beside himself with joy.

He knew he was being rescued.

Chapter 15

"We can judge the heart of a man by his treatment of animals." -- Immanuel Kant

Knowing that Rusty was inside, warm and well fed -- I relaxed into a deep sleep. Tonya said that he was sent with four cans of dog food and his arthritis candies. The next day she took him to be groomed. They bathed him and cut off a lot of his hair because it was very matted; her friend Deidre took him to the vet where he was diagnosed as "underweight, malnourished, dehydrated and abused."

The "dehydrated" diagnosis was probably due to the fact that his water was dirty and he probably refused to drink it. A neighbor said that one of her daughters, and a lady who lived around the corner, were "sneaking food" to him.

This was a twelve year old dog with arthritis sleeping outside on cold concrete. What would Dad think?

I spoke to Deidre on the phone. At first she had wanted to take him to her home. Then it was discovered that Rusty hadn't been neutered, and she said that it would be impossible to keep him with her other male dogs. She also said that he had a microchip and there was evidence that "he had been in a shelter." This caused her to panic. Why, I do not know. I was his legal owner and if the microchip had been scanned, it would have shown my contact information.

She spoke as if this were proof that he was some sort of stolen property or, at the very least, something seriously untoward had taken place.

This wasn't actually said, but her angry and accusatory tones, made me feel that way.

Maybe one day someone will explain to me why the discovery of that microchip was a problem. If they don't, it's okay, because my gratitude towards Deidre and the vet -- far outweighs my curiosity.

She was extremely upset. Because I felt her love for dogs and her desire to help, I tried my best to ignore the anger in her voice. She also added that he was sick because I had given him "tainted vitamins." This was not true. First of all, I hadn't given him *any* vitamins; he only had his candy with the arthritis medicine in it.

She also informed me that Tonya had spent fifty dollars getting Rusty groomed. Her tone of voice became louder, angrier and more abrasive. During this phone call, Howard said that he could hear her voice from the other side of the room. It made me feel as if she didn't seem to realize that I was part of the rescue effort, had offered to pay for Rusty's maintenance and was about to say goodbye to my beloved best friend.

I was in a state of deep sadness and this woman was yelling at me.

After the phone call, I immediately went online to do some research. I found out that a product from the brand, I was using, had been recalled. It was not the candy I had given Rusty and furthermore, the recalled product was not even sold in New York State.

There was another voicemail from Cara. She demanded to know: "where is Rusty -- is he coming back, we don't know anything."

I did not respond. A response would come later; I was too busy trying to find Rusty a real home.

I was not feeling any anger. In my reality, I had no frame of reference for dealing with people who were unkind to animals. One day, shortly after I first met her, Cara mentioned that she had heard that my sister Dolores "spoiled" her pets. I ignored that remark. What I could not ignore was watching her in my Dad's house rearranging the furniture, getting rid of things and redecorating. This behavior shocked me. I immediately called my sister Florence, and after a quick discussion, moved everything back. Yes, Cara and my brother had given me some uncomfortable stares – but I didn't care.

At the time, my Dad was still alive.

Every day, as usual, the neighborhood children showed up to play with Rusty at the gate. One afternoon, I noticed Cara's daughter standing next to him.

As I watched, she told them: "leave my dog alone."

Chapter 16

"I love to think of nature as an unlimited broadcasting station, through which God speaks to us every hour, if we will only tune in." -- George Washington Carver

I decided that it was time for a visit to a nearby lake. I needed to experience the healing power of nature. Walking over I thought: "I hope I see some deer." The law of attraction must have been listening because I was quickly presented with direct evidence of its workings.

First I sat under a tree and, as usual, leaned against it. A little brown dog ran up to me and jumped onto my lap. I was petting it until the owner called it away. He thought his dog was bothering me. I, on the other hand, enjoyed the brief visit and would've been happy to hold him longer.

As I sat there absorbing the 'tree energy,' I looked at the lake and felt very sad. Suddenly I was not alone. I looked around and there were deer on both sides of me. They were all sizes, young and old. I counted and there were nine of them!

After they left, I drew a card from Doreen Virtue's *Magical Messages from the Fairies* deck. On it was a picture of a reindeer and the word "Travel" was written beneath it. How incredible and comforting to see this animal on a card minutes after being surrounded by deer!

The card said: "An upcoming trip proves to be life-changing in positive ways."

This particular tree was not chosen at random. I often sit under it to pray, meditate or just read my fairy or angel cards. While sitting under it, I've had a butterfly touch my face and fly away -- a dragonfly light on my leg, fly away, return and actually sit on my chest while looking up at my face. And yes there have been other days when deer were near me – but never nine at one time.

Since I've always enjoyed a special kinship with animals, I was sure that these visits were all part of a larger plan. They were being affectionate -- while lending me their light and support.

At least, that's how it felt.

My next call from Deidre really floored me. She said that she had dropped Rusty off at the Town of North Hempstead Animal Shelter in Port Washington. In a state of panic, I asked: "What if they euthanize him?" She said it was a "no kill" shelter and that she didn't "believe in any other kind." She said that she had removed his collar and told the receptionist that she'd found him on Main Street. I was to call, claim him and tell them that he ran away from me at the Mill Pond.

I was more than upset.

I thought about how frightened, abandoned and lonely Rusty must have felt. I called Tonya and asked why he wasn't placed in a kennel or a hotel for dogs. She said "because that costs $500 a night and I don't think you can afford it!"

She told me to be prepared for questions about why he was so thin. I do not think that she had any prior knowledge of her friend's plan, but she knew what had been done and told me to leave Deidre's name out of any conversations that I would have with the shelter because she could "get into a lot of trouble."

My only concern was to get Rusty *out* of trouble.

Chapter 17

"The highest realms of thought are
impossible to reach without first allowing an
understanding of compassion." -- Socrates

I immediately called the shelter and was sent directly to voicemail. The next day when I woke up, I called my sister Florence and had a complete meltdown.

I couldn't stop crying.

It was all too much. On one hand I was being forced to give Rusty away, and on the other I was beginning to feel abused myself. My pride got in the way – or maybe it was my religious upbringing. I had been ordered to call these people and tell them that Rusty was there – because *I* had lost him!

I was left with no choice. The call was made.

The lady who answered was very nice. After I described him, she said that he was there and laughingly described him as "scruffy." She said, since she now knew his name, he would be given a name tag. I was told that the bill for their services would include: his board, medical checkup, shots and a new license. She added that weather permitting, he would be outside during the day and inside at night.

A woman named Jennifer called and said that she was interested in foster parenting him. This was the best and most concrete offer that I'd gotten. She said that she and her husband had assisted shelters in two states and that they owned a female dog. I expressed my concern about Rusty being a male. Jennifer's response was: "Don't worry -- if he bothers her, she'll slap him." My guess was she had ample evidence to back this fact up and she sounded very nice. My next question was: "what if I don't get him a permanent home right away?" She excused herself from the phone to confer with her husband. I heard him say "we wouldn't throw him out." She picked up the phone and assured me that I had nothing to worry about.

Jennifer said that, the following Sunday, she would be volunteering at a pet shelter near my home. The plan was for me to meet her there so that she could take Rusty home. I was happy because he would be living near me and I might be able to visit him. Also this would give me time to figure out whether or not I could move somewhere –to a place that accepted pets -- and get him back.

I was planning to ask one of Dad's friends if they could drive Rusty to the shelter so that I could deliver him to Jennifer and her husband.

My sister Dolores emailed me, again, to remind me that she would send money for Rusty's transportation.

Dolores lives in California and has two dogs. I knew about kennels because when she travels, her pets stay in them or she checks them into pet motels. They even go to church for the Blessing of the Animals which is celebrated in remembrance of St. Francis of Assisi, The Patron Saint of Animals.

She truly loves dogs. Her reason for not taking Rusty was that, in his physical condition, no veterinarian would authorize a plane trip.

During this time, I had a dream about Rusty and Dad. They were both in Heaven. Rusty was facing Dad and talking to him. It was very clear that Rusty was updating him about his treatment since Dad's transition.

It was an intense conversation.

I took a photo of Rusty and attached pictures of two archangels on either side of it. One was Archangel Raphael and the other Archangel Ariel. Raphael's name means "it is God who heals" and Archangel Ariel is called "The Lioness of God." She is a guardian and healer of animals; Archangel Raphael heals them as well.

I created this collage to remind myself that Rusty was surrounded by angels, had their protection and would be restored to health.

Saint Francis was invoked and twice -- with my spiritual sight -- I had a beautiful vision of Jesus carrying Rusty in his arms. He held him in a gentle manner. It was much like the way artists depict him holding a little lamb.

It was a sweet vision.

Chapter 18

"The greatness of a nation and its moral progress can be measured by the way in which its animals are treated."– Mahatma Gandhi

I opened the computer and saw an email from Tonya. The subject was: GREAT NEWS! She wrote: "a woman by the name of Darcy who's based in Linden, New Jersey has found a very nice couple who are very interested in adopting Rusty. They have an older dog and want a companion and are responsible and caring dog owners. I think this is the best solution and we should do whatever it takes to make it happen. They live in Linden, New Jersey and would drive out to the shelter and see if he gets along with their dog.

Please call Darcy asap to discuss, I think this is Rusty's best interest, he needs a stable "forever" home." She added Darcy's email address and phone number and said that she had given my contact information to Darcy as well.

Her email concluded with the words: "This could be it!"

This was great news. At the same time I felt as if my body was saying to my spirit, "this is important, you take care of it – I cannot watch. I'll rejoin you later." When I called Tonya, I must have sounded spacey, with this attitude, because she interrupted my zoned out chatting and sternly said "call her."

I did not have to make the call. Darcy had already contacted the couple to give them Tonya's email address. Tonya, in turn, forwarded copies of everyone's emails to me.

Enter Nicole DeCostello Cole.

I received a copy of an email sent by Nicole. She introduced herself and said that she and her husband had been informed that Rusty was in Port Washington. Since the referral had come from a shelter near them in New Jersey, she assumed that they would be picking him up there. This new information caused a slight change in their plans, but she added: "we are hoping to still meet him but aren't sure right now when that might be."

She then stated her most important concern. "My question to you is if you know about Rusty's temperament. Do you know if he was good with other dogs?" She also wanted to know if he was "playful and active" or one of those "calm comfortable dogs." She concluded with: "I know he's old but that's okay with us."

Tonya's response to Nicole was:

"I am so excited that you are interested in adopting Rusty. He is a very special dog.

I only spent one night with him, here's what I know about his temperament. He is very friendly, walked very well on the leash and when we encountered other dogs in the hallway of my building and on the street he was very good with them, his tail was wagging and was interested in sniffing, etc. In fact, we met a yorkie puppy in front of the coffee shop yesterday and he was so gentle and sweet with her and he's a much bigger dog! He was also affectionate with me, liked attention and to be around people. I didn't see him be playful at all but had good energy, not hyperactive, just happy & excited to go out on a walk. He doesn't pace a lot, he was happy to lay near me when I was on the computer or phone. He did seem to tire a bit at the end of a long walk, as you know he is a senior and probably has some arthritis in his hips.

I encourage you to visit him in the shelter and maybe they will let you take him for a walk or meet your dog. He's truly wonderful, if I could have a dog I would take him in a heartbeat. I am copying Cindy on this e-mail, he was her father's dog and she could give you more information on Rusty.

Thank you so much...I really hope this works out, he's had a rough few months and to get a good home would be a happy ending for this great guy."

Reading this, I thought how wonderful it was that Rusty and Tonya had instantly bonded. I remembered her saying that he was excited and happy to be put in her car and driven away. According to her, he was an excited bundle of pure, furry joy! Recalling this made me very happy. It also reminded me of the times I was actually afraid that some stranger would one day take Rusty away in a car.

I felt this way because he was so loving, approachable and popular.

Thinking about her observation of his gentleness with a smaller dog reminded me of the time when he was sitting near an injured bird. The bird could only hop around. Rusty didn't make any attempt to harm it -- he just calmly watched.

I phoned Nicole. The first thing I noticed was that she had one of the most beautifully modulated voices that I have ever heard. She said that she was carrying Rusty's picture everywhere and constantly thinking about him. She added that, instead of Port Washington, it would be more convenient to pick him up in Brooklyn because it was "just over the bridge" from their home in New Jersey.

She was concerned about him not being neutered and said that maybe it didn't need to be done "because of his age." Her plan was to speak with her vet as she did not wish to create any problems for her female dog.

At the same time, I was thinking "if this doesn't work I'll have ask someone to pick him up for Jennifer." She had called a couple of times to check on his status and I was very happy to know that she was still interested in giving him a temporary home.

My sister Florence contacted her friend Joe, and he agreed to pick me and Rusty up if we needed a ride back to Brooklyn.

I called Nicole and told her that the supervisor at the shelter said that Rusty would get his shots, be neutered and issued a new license. This news made her very happy. She said that because of her excitement and preoccupation with Rusty, her husband had advised her to calm herself down by going for a walk.

Her mind was made up. Rusty was going to join her family. She had even greeted her husband, holding his picture next to her face and saying to it: "Say hello to Daddy."

When I answered Tonya's email, I wrote: "Yes...I think this is it. She's as crazy about him as I am and they haven't even met yet!!! (Rusty's love energy knows no bounds)."

Nicole also asked me if the shelter knew that Rusty was twelve years old. Her veterinarian said that he could take blood tests before being neutered and that would decide whether or not he qualified for the procedure. Somewhere in all this, the shelter decided that they were not going to have him neutered because he had been claimed. They even told me to come and get him – "the sooner the better." They weren't trying to be unkind -- they just thought that he would want to get back home.

This part of his journey was about to be over -- Nicole definitely wanted him.

I updated Tonya with all of this information and wrote: "I'm a mess and sad too...so please understand...this is the hardest thing I've ever had to do. Will write you back soon."

I decided to pick Rusty up and take him back to Dad's house in Brooklyn so that he could say goodbye to his friends and family. I thought that Nicole and her husband could pick him up from there. Since I would be with him, he would definitely be allowed to stay inside.

I thought it was a good plan.

I was wrong.

Chapter 19

"Wisdom is learning what to overlook."--William James

Tonya voiced her disapproval about Rusty returning to the house in Brooklyn; she graciously invited me to spend the night at her home with him instead. Even though I knew that I would be with him and no one would bother him or force me to leave him outside -- I decided that bringing him back there was not a good idea after all. I realized, on many levels, it would not be pleasant for Rusty or me.

In fact, returning there could actually frighten him.

I called the shelter to discuss picking him up and the man who answered the phone asked me to hold on. Then he returned and said that a friend of mine had called and reported that I was taking Rusty out of there to return him to the home where he had been abused. Deidre had done this. She had, obviously, not heard that my plans had changed. He concluded the conversation by telling me that I would have to call back the following Monday and explain my plans to the supervisor.

I imagined that somehow, I might not be allowed to pick up my dog.

I had never met Deidre in person, and while I appreciated the fact that she was helping Rusty – she lied about being a "friend" of mine and had absolutely no authority to make that call.

For my part, I was beyond angry. I called Deidre and started screaming! "How dare she do this? Anyone who really knew me would never believe that someone actually accused me of doing anything that could harm him." She screamed back that she did what she did because she "saw the dog" and this was the reason that she was so passionate and protective.

I had held back when she had spoken to me with so much anger, bossiness and presumptuousness – but this was the last straw!

I have never spoken to anyone like that before and I hope to never scream at anyone again. This was my dog-little brother-child-muse-best friend; I was not going to allow anyone to accuse me of hurting him. She meant well -- but her methods were certainly questionable. If I am ever in trouble, I would definitely want someone like her on my side -- but all of this was leading up to me having to let Rusty go -- and my intense feeling of deep sadness was all the drama I could handle.

When I told Tonya what her friend had done, she said that she had already spoken to her and expressed her disapproval of the phone call made to the shelter.

Shortly after, I wrote a letter to Deidre, thanking her for all the good that she had done for Rusty. She didn't respond and it really didn't matter. Drama aside, she played an important part in his rescue and all I needed was for her to know that, on his behalf and mine, -- I was grateful.

Meanwhile Jennifer called to confirm that she was coming to the local shelter the following weekend. She said, if I could get Rusty there, she would take him home. Once more, she reassured me that I had nothing to worry about –- there would be no time limit on his stay.

I tried to call Tonya to discuss Jennifer's offer but somehow wires got crossed. This ended up being beneficial because at the same time Nicole was making definite plans to bring him home forever, so temporary foster care would no longer be necessary.

I knew that Nicole would need to see if Rusty was compatible with them and their dog -- so until that was done, I was not willing to dismiss Jennifer's offer of foster care.

I still had to wait until after the weekend to call the shelter and explain my position to the supervisor. I called back and she was very gracious. There was no problem – I was still welcome to come and claim my dog.

Chapter 20

"Love animals. God has given them the rudiments of thought and joy untroubled."- Fyodor Dostoyevsky

We decided that I would take the train to Port Washington to pick Rusty up and Tonya would meet us there at 1:00PM. I went shopping and bought some dog food to take with me.

I started to get ready for the trip.

I was so nervous and sad that I decided to go over to the lake. When I arrived, I saw some geese. Most of them were tricolored Canadian. The one exception was a totally white domestic goose that Howard had named Alexander. He had become my favorite. I called out "Alexander, come here" and he waddled over to me. This surprised me since I had never called him over to me before. I had simply admired him from a distance.

When he first showed up, he seemed to be shy; we never saw him near any of the other geese. Then one day I heard him honking loudly. As he stood aside like a drill sergeant, all the other geese stopped eating grass, formed a straight line and marched back into the lake.

He was now in charge.

After our brief visit, I walked to the other side of the lake and sat down under my favorite tree. Soon two deer and a fawn arrived and the fawn stood about six feet away from me.

Sometimes the little ones look at me as if to ask "what are you?" I am always happy to see them because they are so graceful and cute.

After about forty-five minutes, I returned home. Later that evening I decided to work with cards from Doreen Virtue's *Daily Guidance from Your Angels Oracle Cards*. This time I drew a card entitled "Time to Go." It said: "The sun sets and rises each day, and it's the same with the avenues in your life. See the beauty within each sunset in your life, and know that the sun will also rise again tomorrow. Endings are merely the start of a new beginning, and we are with you through each phase and cycle." It went on to say: "Work very closely with your angels during this transition to ensure its harmony for everyone concerned. Surrender any guilt or other negative emotions to heaven as your energy needs to stay high right now." I was advised to "call upon Archangel Azrael for help with grieving and Archangel Michael for help with courage."

Yes, there was guilt because I couldn't keep him. There was deep sadness too.

I was giving away my best friend.

I was supposed to call Tonya to discuss details about picking me and Rusty up -- but I absolutely couldn't talk about this. I emailed her and told her that I was too "choked up" to speak. I also told her that with all that was about to happen, I was sincerely hoping that I could contain my emotions and not make anyone feel uncomfortable the next day when they came to take Rusty to their home.

Later that evening, I received this email from Nicole:

"Cindy, please know that tomorrow should be a happy day for Rusty will be entering his furever home. Like I said, I'll provide plenty of pictures of Rusty "growing up" with us so you'll get to see him often through pictures. We can't wait to take care of him and to meet him. I understand that you are sad but please cheer up. I promise Rusty will be happy, taken care of, and you will not be forgotten. Looking forward to tomorrow. Nicole"

Since I was traveling from upstate New York and the shelter was about ninety miles away, on Long Island, I decided to get up early. There would be a bus ride, then a subway, ending with a train ride. I wanted to get there much earlier than

Tonya's pick up time so that I could have more time to spend alone with Rusty.

I had moments of thinking "I cannot do this!" Where would the strength come from?

Where had it always come from?

I called Silent Unity and asked them for prayer support. I explained some of the background and what I had to do. I was in deep emotional pain and didn't know how I could go through with it. They gave me some words of encouragement and prayed out loud for me. They said that they would continue to pray, about this situation, every day for the next 30 days.

I hung up and immediately fell asleep.

The next morning when I woke up, my perspective had done a complete shift. I heard myself saying: "I'm not giving him away – I'm sharing him." Somehow that idea was both healing and strengthening.

I was ready to face the day.

Chapter 21

"What wisdom can you find that is greater
than kindness?" -- Jean-Jacques Rousseau

I got off the train in Port Washington and felt waves of nostalgia for this pretty little seaside town. I had lived there for ten years as a child and the experience was magical. I loved living in a town with two beaches, a duck pond and a lake for ice skating. We lived on a quiet street opposite a beautiful forest. I spent many hours exploring that forest and going down to the sand banks behind it, usually accompanied by very first pet – a gentle Welsh corgi named Laddie.

The air felt crisp and clean. I quickly looked around Main Street to see if any of the buildings were recognizable, and then found a taxi. The trip to the shelter took about five minutes. I identified myself and they took me outside where Rusty was in a cage. I wrapped my fingers around the bars and he quickly licked them to say hello. Then he stepped back and barked loudly. This was his way of saying: "Get me out of here!"

I paid the bill, picked up copies of his medical report and left a donation. Another thing I was given was his collar and leash. I asked "where did this come from" and was told that a woman had dropped it off. Apparently Deidre had a change of heart and decided to tell the shelter the truth about why and how she had Rusty.

All of my angst, about being forced to lie, was for nothing. Now I was in the presence of people who knew that I had not told the truth about how I'd "lost" him. The lady smiled as she handed these two items over to me. She had probably heard all kinds of stories before and, ultimately, all I felt from her and Deidre was their deep love for these precious animals.

Rusty was by my side -- well fed, groomed and safe. That is all that really mattered.

During our first hour together, he did a lot of whimpering and I tried my best to comfort him. I hugged him and even chanted softly.

We walked over a bridge and he jumped up on the railing. I had no idea what was happening. I threw my arms around him and pulled him back down. The idea of him jumping off of that bridge threw me into serious, panic mode. I later realized that he heard the sound of water flowing under the bridge and wanted to drink some. When we walked away, he drank rain water that had formed a pool on the path.

At one point he looked up the hill and saw other dogs in cages. He wanted to visit with them so he pulled me in their direction. They became angry and started barking. This time I did the pulling and we walked back down the hill. I found a picnic table and we sat there waiting for Tonya's arrival.

Even though Rusty had only been with her for a short time, when she drove down the hill, he jumped up as if he recognized her car. We were both happy to see her. After saying "hello" and formally introducing ourselves, I offered her one hundred dollars for his expenses. She refused it with the explanation of "I wanted to help." We did decide that I could, at least, give her $20.00 for gas money.

I will never forget her generosity.

Tonya said that the shelter was supposed to send Rusty home with a bag of dog food. I went back to the office to collect it. As I walked away, Rusty got upset and I heard her say: "she's coming back."

I was given a large bag of dog food and we got into the car. At first Rusty had his head out the window. Then he lay down on the seat and immediately fell asleep. I had never seen him sleep in a car before.

We arrived at Tonya's apartment. She had made a bed for him and there was a bowl of water near it. We ordered lunch from a nearby macrobiotic restaurant. Since I'd been up since 4:00AM I was very sleepy and decided to take a short nap.

Later on we noticed that Rusty was walking with a limp. Tonya asked "how far did you walk him?" We had not walked far -- there wasn't enough space for a long walk. He had simply been separated from his medicine for a few days. I gave him a couple of pieces of his arthritis candy and he was soon walking normally.

I got down on my knees to pet Rusty and he began nuzzling me and I started hugging him. I felt that this was his way of showing love and gratitude for being rescued after enduring so much abuse.

On all of my previous visits, we always had lots of hugging and nuzzling moments. This one was different - it would end with goodbye.

Rusty was staring at his makeshift bed. It had a lump in the middle. I smoothed it out and he immediately sat down.

Tonya had made him feel perfectly at home.

She received a call from Nicole saying that they were on the way and would call when they were about to cross the bridge. This would be our signal to go outside and wait.

While we were waiting we went to the computer and googled Nicole. One fact stood out: her birthday was September 10th which was the exact same date as my conversation with Doreen Virtue on Hay House Radio. It could be said that Doreen's Angel Therapy® reading was the official start of my search for a new home for Rusty! She said that she had a "hit" that there was a family out there that would take him. Now they were on their way to do just that.

We were googling Nicole for fun as we already knew that Rusty was going to a good home with nice, highly recommended, pet loving people. I had already done a little research on my own. I found out that she was a lawyer in private practice, and that she and members of her firm had built a house for Habitat for Humanity. She had taken the time to help build a house! Now, that was clearly a you-had-me-at-hello-moment.

The call came. We went outside to wait. A neighbor came by and asked: "Is that Rusty?" Then another neighbor asked the same question. Apparently Tonya had really put the word out about him. One of the neighbors was sitting on her bicycle looking at him. All of a sudden, in a shocked tone of voice, she said: "he's peed in the shape of the infinity sign." I looked and it was roughly in the shape of a figure eight. How did he make that happen? Wow. Rusty, were you trying to tell me something in your unusual but magical way?

Nicole, her husband Pete and their dog Nika arrived. We were in the presence of two beautiful young people and a very cute Dutch Keeshond dog.

Pete was carrying a bowl and a bottle of water for Rusty. He poured it out and put it on the ground. Rusty immediately lapped it up. Nika was saying "hello" by sniffing him. Then she walked away, turned around, and looked him over some

more. Pete laughed and said "she thinks she's being traded."
We were meeting outside to see if the two dogs got along.
They did.

We decided to take a walk around the block.

Pete and I walked side by side and I held Rusty on the leash.
Nicole, Tonya and Nika walked behind us. He told me that,
like his wife, he was a lawyer. We talked about his practice and
after a short while, I handed the leash over to him. He looked
at me with a combination of sympathy and gratitude.

I had purchased a camera on the way out to Port Washington.
After handing the leash over to Pete, I walked behind them
and took a picture of Pete and Rusty walking together for
the first time.

That was the first part of my good bye and it would be a long
time before I would send a copy of this particular photo to
Nicole.

They also brought a camera and we took lots of pictures
outside. I could see that Rusty was perfectly comfortable
around them and Nika. After our walk around the block, we
went inside, took more pictures, and talked.

Pete said that they had adopted another dog from the shelter
and when they got it home it was foaming at the mouth. Four
days later it was gone.

I gave them a copy of Rusty's medical report. He had age
related arthritis, but nothing else to be concerned about. They

told me that he would be added to Nika's health insurance policy and given the same prescription medicine that she was taking. Another plan was to have the two dogs groomed on the same day.

I didn't know if they were intuitive or if Tonya had told them how Rusty had been barred from one room after the other in his former home -- but Nicole made a point of telling me that he would be welcome to stay in every single room in their house, and that he would only be outside when they were with him. She added that they intended to have a fence built the following summer.

All of a sudden Pete walked over to me and gave me a hug; Nicole hugged me too. I knew what that meant.

I didn't want to let him go.

I had no choice. I gave them a bag with a couple of cans of dog food and a package of his arthritis candy. Everything was going smoothly and my wish of not wanting to make anyone uncomfortable seemed to be coming true – until those goodbye hugs.

They were all heading towards the door. I couldn't put one foot in front of the other to join them. I said "I can't do this part." Tonya let me know that it was alright to remain inside and I watched her, Pete and Nicole walk out the door. I didn't look down so I didn't actually see Rusty leave. I rushed into the bathroom and started crying. I remembered the angel card reading and cried out to Archangel Michael and Archangel Azrael to give me strength and heal my grief. A couple of minutes later, the tears abruptly stopped.

I had no more tears to shed. The archangels had come through.

By the time Tonya returned, I had calmed down. I asked her what happened and she said that she had helped them "load him into the car." He was now on his way to his new home -- to what Nicole called his "furever" home.

A half hour later, I was on my way home.

The next day, I received an email from Nicole with eighteen pictures of Rusty attached. The caption said "Adopting Rusty." I was so happy to receive them. Still reading the word "adopting" made me feel a little sad; also Rusty looked confused, tired and lonely. When I described his appearance to my sister Florence, she said she always thought he had "a puzzled look on his face."

What he actually had now was a loving family and a beautiful new home.

Every night before going to sleep, I remembered to say a prayer of gratitude for this blessed turn of events.

I contacted Jennifer to let her know that Rusty had been adopted. She was very happy to hear this. I will always be grateful to Jennifer and her husband for their generous offer to be Rusty's foster parents.

Two weeks after Rusty left for his new home, I decided to call Dad's friends in Brooklyn to let them know about his adoption.

I called the next door neighbors first. Dad's friend Winston said that Sunshine, the other dog, had died and they didn't know what had happened to Rusty. I explained his whereabouts and he was very happy to hear about Rusty's good fortune. Later I spoke to his wife Pat and she was grateful to hear the news as well. She told me that one morning she "woke up and Rusty was gone." No one explained his whereabouts and she didn't "feel comfortable asking." As she spoke to me, she continuously spoke of God's grace and praised Him for Rusty's rescue. She added that people had been knocking on her door to find out what had happened to him.

I told them both about his new home. They were happy to hear that he was with a responsible and caring family who would take good care of him. I called one more neighbor and between these two large and loving families, I knew that the rest of the neighborhood would soon hear the good news. I promised to send them pictures of him in his new environment -- and I did.

Chapter 22

"Pets are wonderful friends and teachers who teach us a lot about unconditional love -- about healthy boundaries too!" --Narmada Akshat

Nicole sent pictures of Rusty at a barbeque. He looked clean, healthy and comfortable. I felt that he still looked a little confused – but he was safe, warm and protected. A psychoanalyst might say that my assessment of his emotional state was based on my sadness and that I was simply "projecting."

I soon received another email that said Rusty had been taken to Petsmart ®. for the first time. I don't know if they took him there to buy food, see the vet or be groomed. I do know that she said he enjoyed himself.

She added that he was finishing up the arthritis candy that I had sent along with him and was about to be given the same prescription medicine as Nika. They were worried when they noticed a worm in his stool. The vet gave him a dose of medicine at once and they were waiting for the test results.

Fortunately, the vet said that administering the medicine right away, would be the beginning of the cure.

My prayers of gratitude, for the care that they were giving Rusty, were being answered in every email!

She also wrote that whenever they put him in the car he cried. This was understandable since he had been in two cars with nice people, who handed him over to others. He was afraid that he was going to be given away again. We both realized that time would take care of this fear – and it did.

The best news came in the email that had the subject: "Rusty has gained 4 pounds." I, in turn, emailed this news to his friends, fans and family!

She also told me that he had a sleepover at her parents and her four year old nephew was there. He had gotten along with everyone and the little boy was especially thrilled to spend the night with him. None of this came as a surprise to me. The night we met, I told them that Rusty seemed to especially enjoy playing with little boys. I remembered how Pete's face lit up as he told me about his nephew.

I was also told that he was leaning on them, flipping over for belly rubs and wrestling with Pete. My Sweet Puppito was happy once more.

So was I.

Thanks to Nicole and her emails and photos, I still felt connected to him.

I sent some of the pictures to my friend Janice Fotopoulos. She was one of Rusty's biggest fans and one of the people who would ask me how I was feeling in one breath and quickly add "how is Rusty" in the next. People like Janice had never met him but from my descriptions of him, they could feel his sweet energy. Her email response to the pictures was:

Hi Cindy,

I was able to view these photos that you sent me. Rusty looks so happy. It looks like he got a great home too. I am very happy for both of you because I know that although it was very hard for you to let him go, you found him an awesome home and a place to be loved and cared for which is more than any dog could ever ask for. Be at peace knowing that he is in a good place and that you can visit him. Talk to you soon.

Love,

Janice

Janice always owns dogs. She volunteers at a pet shelter, sends monthly donations, and is truly a lover of animals. Her note really uplifted me.

Another email from Nicole contained some very good news too:

Hi Cindy & Tonya,

I took some pictures of Rusty and Nika last night to give you an update.

Rusty is now a whopping 58 pounds. He has gained ten pounds and I think he's now at a healthy weight that we can keep him at. He's better at taking his treats and has learned to be gentle with his food. He got a bath two weeks ago and did well there, although they told me he was a little afraid of the water. I'm going to be taking them for Santa pictures within the next two weeks so be on the look-out for those. Hope you're well.

Nicole

Knowing how wonderful Nicole was about keeping her promises, I couldn't wait to see the Christmas pictures.

The pictures were emailed to me a week before Christmas. They were on a postcard that played a very upbeat version of "Deck the Halls with Boughs of Holly." It said it was a message from Rusty. I've sent cards and signed his name. He's received cards from other dogs. So a Christmas card signed by him was no surprise. It said: "Happy Holidays from Rusty and his Family."

In the photographs, Rusty was wearing antlers. In one he was looking at the ground, while Nika looked straight ahead as if she were born to be a Christmas card model. Another picture showed Rusty looking up; Nicole and Pete, exuding radiance and joy, were holding both dogs.

After Christmas, I received more pictures.

There were pictures of Rusty opening a Christmas present. It was a veggie bone – one of his favorite treats. In other pictures, he was carrying the bone all over the house, having breakfast with Pete, hanging out with his sister and being embraced by Nicole.

As much as I loved sharing his Christmas through all of these pictures, I must admit that I felt a tinge of sadness and jealousy when I saw Nicole hugging him. Then I got back into my right mind and realized that she was hugging him for me! After all, one of my favorite pictures, taken the night they met, was one of her hugging him for the first time.

I emailed some copies of the photos to my cousin Marsha Bennett. She wrote back that seeing the Christmas stocking with Rusty's name on it "brought a tear" to her eye. She truly loved him. After his rescue, she and her employer had made a contribution, on his behalf, to an organization that forwards donations to animal shelters. She had checked their list and found out that they shared funds with the shelter that had housed him in Port Washington.

Looking at those beautiful pictures, I felt as if I had received the greatest Christmas present of all.

The light had come back into Rusty's eyes.

Chapter 23

"If you don't have a dog--at least one--there is not necessarily anything wrong with you, but there may be something wrong with your life."-- Vincent van Gogh

My wish is that anyone, who has to find a home for a pet, is fortunate enough to place them with animal lovers such as Nicole and Pete.

They generously kept me involved by sending photographs and emails. I shared many of the photos with Rusty's friends, fans and "relatives." Like me, they were happy to see him living in comfort, surrounded by love.

In one group of pictures Rusty was covered by what looked like a gray sweat shirt. This was done because the boiler had broken and they wanted to make sure that he was warm.

He looked very cute.

The same email contained pictures of a trip that the family had taken to a beach in Delaware. The first one showed Pete walking the two dogs down the boardwalk. Nika was ahead of him and Rusty was behind. I was wondering if he was staying back out of fear. This thought did not last long because in the next picture he was walking straight into the ocean. Pete had to quickly take off his shoes to keep up with him.

The pictures were beautiful.

While Rusty was living in Brooklyn, there were no trips to the ocean, and the first time we ever walked through a forest together was when I picked him up at the shelter in Port Washington.

I loved seeing him at the ocean.

An email with several pictures arrived in September. I was thinking that a celebration was coming up soon because it would be Rusty's one year anniversary with his new family -- an entire year living in the place that Nicole referred to as "his furever home."

The pictures were beautiful. He and his sister looked like "Team Puppy Dogs" – born to be together. There was a glow about them. I especially loved a picture of the two of them standing side by side, and it quickly became the wallpaper on my desktop computer. Nika looked radiant, and I made a mental note to write to Nicole and tell her how much I loved these particular pictures of Rusty's sister.

There was a picture of Rusty sitting next to Pete and a couple of him relaxing in his white doggy bed. I smile when I think of that because I had received pictures of him sitting on at least three different beds. The smile comes because when we first met at Tonya's house, Pete had joked about how many of these beds Nicole had placed throughout their home.

I think he may have said: seven.

I emailed some of the pictures to my family with the subject: "The Latest Pictures of My Sweet Puppito."

By now Nicole had sent me 139 pictures.

I was more than grateful and every night, I continued to thank God for Rusty's wellbeing and new life.

One night, I dreamt of him flying through the air and landing on someone's terrace in New York City. I guess I could interpret that as seeing that he had truly made a safe landing.

In another dream, I was at a beach with Rusty, Nicole and Pete. We were all very happy and I got to pet Rusty over and over.

The next morning, I woke up grateful for having the gift of lucid dreaming.

First thing in the morning I started telepathically talking to him and was actually hearing his answers. I know that some people have said that animal responses come as feelings – but, in my mind, I was hearing his responses as complete sentences.

I kept this information to myself.

It would be awhile before I discovered that other people communicated with animals; some do this professionally and are well known. Two that come to mind are: Michelle Childery of the United Kingdom and Karen Anderson of the United States. They are both known as "animal communicators."

They contact animals telepathically, do readings, find lost pets, write books on the subject, -- and have been featured on many television shows.

I had, after all, called Doreen Virtue on the air saying that I knew that she could "tune in" to Rusty. She did - and gave a reading that proved to be 100% accurate.

Strangely enough, there was no fear involved in my decision to keep my telepathic conversations with Rusty to myself. The thought of sharing this information just simply never entered my mind.

Chapter 24

"You transform all who are touched by you."-- Rumi

As September 23 approached, I expected to receive one year anniversary pictures of Rusty and Nika. In my imagination, I saw them both wearing party hats, eating treats and having a great time.

Instead, I received this:

Subject: Nika & Rusty

Date: Monday, September 28, 2009, 5:09 PM

Hi Cindy & Tonya,

As you may know, this past week was our one year anniversary with Rusty. It was also unfortunately a very sad day for us with our little girl Nika. She had an attack on Labor Day where her heart ruptured. We did everything we could for her but she passed away on Sept. 23 from the ruptured heart. Rusty is a little bit lonely but is doing alright with us. We're thankful to have him to come home to. Thank you for your thoughts.

Nicole

I shared this news with Rusty's family and friends. My nephew Gerald responded with a one line email: "this is so sad."

Yes it was.

I wrote back to Nicole expressing my sympathy and sharing my belief that "all dogs go to Heaven."

I really loved that little dog. She was there for Rusty and she was there for me. The idea that she could be Rusty's sister and companion meant a lot to me.

It still does.

Christmas arrived. This time, I didn't receive a card with a family portrait. Instead I received pictures of their beautifully decorated home and, of course, Rusty.

They had stockings hanging on the fireplace with the names: Nicole, Pete, Rusty, and Nika – plus two new ones: Griswold and Priscilla.

A large photo of Nika was lovingly displayed on the mantel. I guess she was looking down from Heaven and smiling. Her presence was definitely felt and their home, as usual, looked warm and cozy.

I continued to miss Rusty.

My sister Dolores had told me, in no uncertain terms, that I should not try to visit him. My heart said otherwise - so I decided to discuss it with a professional.

There is a veterinary hospital near my home. One day I saw one of the doctors outside and asked him if he could answer a question.

I told him about Rusty and how the people who adopted him said that I could visit. His response was also "no." He said that visiting would only confuse and upset him emotionally -- and when I left -- he would have to "readjust once more to his new family."

Surely that was not the answer that I wanted, but it was the answer I needed.

Chapter 25

"The fate of animals is of greater importance to me than the fear of appearing ridiculous; it is indissolubly connected with the fate of man." -- Emile Zola

The following spring I returned to Paris for three weeks. As always, it was great to be back. While visiting one of my favorite parks, I observed a delightful site. A boy around five years old was running with a dog. He held one end of the leash in his hand and the dog held the other end in its mouth. They were both having so much fun. Another joyful aspect of that scene was the fact that the dog was the same color as Rusty!

Even in Paris I continued my mental dialogue with him. He was living one state away from me in America. I didn't give much thought about this until one morning when I mentally greeted him and his response was "where are you?"

I guess he felt the distance.

One of the many reasons that I love Paris is because it is so pet friendly. In some restaurants you see dogs seated beside their owners. Years earlier, when I lived there, I used to shop at a grocery store that had a stand outside for dog leashes. The sign attached to it read: "pour nôtre amis, les bêtes."

This literally means "for our friends, the beasts."

I have owned three other dogs in my life and loved them all, but Rusty had something extra – a very special sweetness. I wrote about this to Nicole and she agreed. She also said that he was patient and stood still even when she was cleaning out his ears.

One of her emails ended with these words: "He is still the sweetest boy ever and we love him dearly."

I remembered how patient he used to be when I gave him baths. He would stand there and calmly let you wash and towel dry him. There was no shaking or trying to escape. My childhood pet, Laddie, would get agitated during a bath and run away as soon as it was over. Then he would wallow in the grass to dry himself – grateful to be out of the tub and as far away from us as possible.

January arrived and I went to work with my friend Lois DiBlasi. Lois had never met Rusty but she counted herself among his fans. Like many others, she fell in love with him because of my stories about his personality and our adventures. After she greeted me, she would always ask: "How is our dog?"

Lois and I had been working together when I first realized that I had to find another home for Rusty. After his adoption, I sent her photographs of him in his new home. She responded with three words: "He looks happy." I continued to share his photos with her, and like others, she began to ask me if I'd received more. My sister Jean was beginning to end phone calls with "how's Rusty?"

I really didn't know. It seemed as if the flow of communication had, somehow, been interrupted.

Lois inquired about him once more, and I repeated that I didn't know what was going on -- and hesitated to ask. Her response to my answer (regarding Nicole) was: "Why are you afraid of her?"

It was not fear. I decided that I did not want to come across as pushy or intrusive. This family rescued my best friend, gave him a loving home and was keeping us together via photos and emails. They had done more than I had ever expected. Their kindness was overwhelming.

I simply did not want to make them feel uncomfortable in any way.

I received an invitation to attend a two day workshop facilitated by Solara-An Ra. Solara teaches fundamental tools for spiritual connection including: breath work, meditation, channeling, grounding and energy awareness.

The worldwide web introduced us and I subsequently joined her mailing list. So naturally, when she came to New York City, I registered for her two day workshop.

My eyes were closed during one of the exercises and, in my mind's eye, I saw violet colored orbs on a black background. The orbs resembled shimmering pearls. There was also something else in the picture. If one could imagine it as a painting -- in the lower right hand corner -- was Rusty!

It was as if he were looking through a window -- into my mind.

I really didn't see anything peculiar about his appearance. After all, I already had visions of Jesus carrying him, we had telepathic conversations, and he and his family had been in my prayers every night for a year and a half.

I simply considered his appearance at the workshop as one more example of our never ending bond.

A couple of weeks after the workshop, Nicole emailed several pictures of Rusty. He looked noticeably different. His hair was longer and whiter. His face looked much older.

This group of pictures introduced me to the new dogs. In one picture Priscilla was sitting next to Rusty. The email said: "she stays by his side and adores him." Her breed was not clear to me. The other dog: Griswold, a male Dutch Keeshond, looked rather cute, fun loving and mischievous.

It didn't surprise me that Priscilla chose to stay by Rusty's side.

In one of the pictures, Rusty's nose was buried in the snow. With snow covered trees behind him and actual snow falling down, I felt as if I were looking at a piece of great artwork. The pictures taken inside, which appeared to have been taken at an earlier date, showed him running around with a veggie bone in his mouth -- looking warm and content.

I quickly forwarded these photos to calm everyone down.

Chapter 26

"Love rests on no foundation. It is an endless ocean, with no beginning or end."--Rumi

One morning I woke up with the idea that I should do something creative with Rusty's collar. (The one that was returned to me at the shelter). It had identification tags on it as well as a few strands of his hair. I had been keeping it in a blue velvet gift box. Thinking that I wanted to openly display it, I decided to place the collar in a deep picture frame with a collage of his photos – to create a beautiful keepsake.

That same day I made up my mind to become a volunteer at a nearby pet shelter. I felt that doing this would lessen the pain of not seeing Rusty and, most importantly, allow me to assist the staff with the animals. Since they accept donations, I added dog food to my shopping list. The plan was to deliver the food and, at the same time, find out how to become a volunteer.

I had recently taken a business course for performers. One of the things we were advised to do, was to read our emails later in the day. The teacher explained that receiving an email usually means that there is something you have to do. She said: "schedule reading them during a period of time when you're willing to respond." This sounded logical so I decided to follow this suggestion; I would open my emails when Howard and I returned home from shopping.

When we walked through the door, the clock said 4:44. I had never seen this numerical sequence on my clock before. I had been told many times that 444 means "the angels are with you." I thought "that's nice" and prepared to put my groceries away.

After a while I decided to go online and check my emails.

I had chosen gmail as my account because it was set up so that it is not necessary to go through news stories in order to get to my messages. They have an option where you can click a drop down menu and select the news if you wish - but you are not forced to read it - and that works for me.

When you open your inbox you see who it is from, the subject, and the first line of the message. This preview sometimes helps me to decide whether or not I wish to read the message immediately or later.

I scanned the list to see who had written me and stopped when I found a message from Tonya. The words on the subject line said how "sad" she felt. There was another one that had been sent earlier from Nicole.

Rusty was gone.

Nicole wrote:

Hi Cindy and Tonya,

I'm sorry to be writing this email and be the bearer of bad news, but I must inform you that our Rusty has passed away and crossed over to the Rainbow Bridge. You may remember my last email to you was that Rusty was going through a rough patch. Well he had a rough two months but he kept pulling through, getting better and responding well to antibiotics. However, he stopped eating about three weeks ago so Pete and I fed him anything we could get him to eat. On Friday he finally stopped wanting everything.. no human food, no treats, nothing. We knew things were getting bad. On Saturday we noticed he was suffering and tried our best to get him to eat something and go outside.

Unfortunately, our efforts didn't do anything. Pete and I made the decision that we would take him to the vet again on Sunday to see what we could do and consider letting him go. We didn't even make it through the night. Rusty started throwing up blood late Saturday night and got really really bad so we decided to rush him to Red Bank Vet Hospital at midnight that night. His blood pressure was only 30 when we arrived at the hospital. We decided to assist Rusty to peace rather than watch him suffer any longer. It was the hardest decision we've ever made. In the car ride down to the hospital, Rusty lifted his head and paid attention to me a bunch of times, which was nice because he hadn't done that all day. I think he knew we were finally letting him go in peace. I rode with him in the backseat and can tell you he was definitely at peace.

Our Rusty was amazing - as we all know - and he tried his best to stay with us as long as he could. In the end, it was the humane thing to do and we said goodbye to him peacefully and lovingly. Rusty will be cremated privately and he'll share our fireplace mantle with our beloved Nika soon. I regret having to inform you of this news. We all know how loving and wonderful Rusty was. I can only thank you both for allowing us to be a part of his life. We are thankful for the time we got to spend with him and thankful that Rusty graced us with his personality.

Pete and I have lost two great dogs in the last six months. While I'll never forget that moment in the hospital of letting him go, I'll also never forget meeting him with both of you at Tonya's. I must close my email now as I'm crying too much.

All the best and with love to Rusty. RIP our Russman.

Nicole

Even though I hadn't received any correspondence regarding Rusty's health, this news did not surprise me. I'd had a vision of him at a spiritual gathering, a month earlier, and I finally emailed Nicole asking for an update. She responded with more pictures -- but I still had an uneasy feeling.

This message explained why.

I decided to call my sister Florence first and deliver the sad news. My voice started out normally and was quickly reduced to a whisper.

The words could not come out.

The next day I sent a quick email to Nicole.

Dearest Nicole,

I received your email; I could not sleep last night. I will write you more later. As you know I've thanked you and Pete a million times and will probably continue to do so.

Thank you for keeping in touch with me and being there for the sweetest puppy dog in the world; he was and still is -- a beautiful "force of nature."

Until next time....

Blessings,

Cindy

A few days later I sent the following email to Nicole, Pete and Tonya:

Dearest Nicole, Pete and Tonya,

Thank you for all that you've done for Rusty.

Such a beautiful spirit deserved to meet the three of you.

I was living at my Dad's house when Rusty showed up. He was living with my niece and her mother. They were moving to a new apartment (and like my present one) pets were not allowed. Dad said that a lady who lived across the street would take him once she had a fence built; twelve years later he was still with us.

My Dad was the oldest person on the block and all of the neighbors revered him and his sidekick: Rusty. Every day at around 3:00 you could hear the voices of little kids shouting "Rusty, Rusty" and he would run out of the side door and greet them. When I called back to let them know that he was living with a family described as "caring and responsible" by the shelter who recommended you -- the neighbors were rejoicing!

He's on my desktop and on my cell and there hasn't been a night (since he moved to NJ) that I've gone to bed without praying a prayer of gratitude that he had safety, love and care....thanks to the three of you. I never felt "disconnected" from him because he was in his wonderful new home -- and receiving all of those emails and pictures helped big time.

The other morning I got up thinking that I have his old collar with its tags (and a little bit of his hair) stored in a velvet gift box and I'll have to somehow do a collage and add that collar to the pictures. Later I thought that one way to lessen the "void" would be to volunteer at a pet shelter. I recently discovered that one (Pets Alive!) is a mile and a half from my house. That way I'd be around lots of pets and I could help out too......so when I went shopping I bought a large bag of dog food to bring over on Saturday........Then I received the news and the events of the day and the recent premonitions made sense...........Now I'm still doing a gratitude prayer with his name in it and I've also prayed that your hearts will heal.

You graciously told me that I could visit him at your house. My sister said "no" and then I had a consultation with a vet and he also said "no" because it would cause Rusty emotional confusion. That certainly wasn't the answer I wanted -- but I had to think of his well being and I knew that his family in New Jersey was giving him lots of love and care and he also had the company of some wonderful dogs --and new relatives -- as well.

I had a few nicknames for Rusty: My Sweet Puppito, The Puppy Dog Love of My Life and one that I called him when I took him to the vet. I told him not to be afraid because he's "GOD'S PUPPY." The vet looked at me as if he were thinking: "wow -- somebody gets it!" Yes I do and fortunately for Rusty...so do you!

With love,

Cindy

Later on I wrote a note to some members of my family explaining that while thanking Rusty's three "earth angels" (Nicole, Pete and Tonya) – I felt the need to share some of his background -- fill them in on his life with Dad and me because it was so different from the way that they found him.

Later I would decide that, truthfully, this one magnificent terrier-chow-angel mix of a dog had experienced two incarnations in one lifetime with two different families.

How lucky we all were.

I took the dog food to Pets Alive and saw several horses and lots of dogs -- dogs being walked on leashes and a corral full of happy, energetic ones. A staff member thanked me for the donation and gave me the schedule for volunteer training.

The whole time I was there, I felt a painful lump in my throat.

Rusty's collar remains in the blue velvet gift box, along with a small amount of his hair that I removed from his hair brush. I do not know if I will ever revive the plan of taking these items out and placing them in a picture frame.

One day I opened the box and found a white feather inside. I did not place it there.

This was a clear sign from the angels.

Chapter 27

"Goodbyes are only for those who love with their eyes. Because for those who love with heart and soul there is no such thing as separation."-- Rumi

The Rainbow Bridge

Just this side of heaven is a place called Rainbow Bridge.

When an animal dies that has been especially close to someone here, that pet goes to Rainbow Bridge.

There are meadows and hills for all of our special friends so they can run and play together.

There is plenty of food, water and sunshine, and our friends are warm and comfortable.

All the animals that had been ill and old are restored to health and vigor; those that were hurt or maimed are made whole and strong again, just as we remember them in our dreams of days and times gone by.

The animals are happy and content, except for one small thing; they each miss someone very special to them, who had to be left behind.

They all run and play together, but the day comes when one suddenly stops and looks into the distance. His bright eyes are intent; His eager body quivers. Suddenly he begins to run from the group, flying over the green grass, his legs carrying him faster and faster.

You have been spotted, and when you and your special friend finally meet, you cling together in joyous reunion, never to be parted again.

The happy kisses rain upon your face; your hands again caress the beloved head, and you look once more into the trusting eyes of your pet, so long gone from your life but never absent from your heart.

Then you cross the Rainbow Bridge together....

--Author Unknown

Rusty,

My Sweet Puppito

We have a date!

Epilogue

Rusty's angels made their presence known to me when I attended an International Angel Day workshop in New York City. That was when Archangel Michael told me, in a channeled message, not to worry because the angels were looking after him.

I didn't understand it then – but I understand it now.

I've learned that synchronicities are reminders that the angels are giving us guidance. This proved to be true on three separate occasions.

First, I attended the above-mentioned workshop on September 10, 2006. Then my on-air conversation with Doreen Virtue, took place two years later on September 10, 2008.

Less than two weeks later, Rusty went to live with Nicole. Her birthday is September 10th!

Thank you angels.

Rusty's story doesn't end here.

A couple of years ago, I decided to do something special on Father's Day in memory of Dad. First, I purchased a helium filled balloon. Then I wrote a message and attached it to the string.

I called my sisters and asked them if I should sign their names on it and they all said "yes."

I wrote: "Dad, we miss you and we love you." Then I had an afterthought and wrote: "P.S. -- If you see Rusty, please give him a hug for me."

It was a beautiful day. The sky was partially cloudy, and it was warm. I walked over to the lake and released the balloon.

I sat on a bench and watched as it gracefully floated up to the sky. Seeing it reach the sky, sail through the clouds and disappear gave me a peaceful and happy feeling.

Later on, in my mind's eye, I saw Dad bending down to catch the balloon as it arrived in Heaven.

Besides my sisters, I hadn't told anyone about releasing our Father's Day balloon.

A few months later, my friend Narmada Akshat, who lives 7300 miles away in India, responded to an email from me. Among other subjects, I had written about finding a feather in the box containing Rusty's belongings.

In his response, he said that he had recently seen Rusty in a vision.

What was our little dog doing?

Rusty was playing with a balloon.

References

A Course in Miracles – Foundation for Inner Peace - www. facim.org

The Bible:

THE HOLY BIBLE, NEW INTERNATIONAL VERSION®, NIV® Copyright © 1973, 1978, 1984, 2011 by Biblica, Inc.™ Used by permission. All rights reserved worldwide - www. biblica.com

King James Version (Public Domain)

Ruiz, don Miguel: *The Four Agreements* published by Amber Allen Publishing – www.amberallen.com

Virtue, Doreen: *Magical Messages from the Fairies Oracle Cards; Daily Guidance from Your Angels Oracle Cards* published by Hay House, Inc. - www.hayhouse.com

Gratitude List

God, Archangels, Angels, Jesus, Saint Francis, Fairies and my Friends in the Animal Kingdom

American Society for the Prevention of Cruelty to Animals
www.aspca.org / (800) 628-0028

Berry Milton Jones III
http://TheAngelSchool.com

David Hoffmeister
www.livingmiraclescenter.org

don Miguel Ruiz, MD
www.newagreementsforlife.com

Doreen Virtue, Ph.D.
www.AngelTherapy.com

Hay House Radio
www.HayHouseRadio.com

James J. Kriegsmann, Jr.
www.kriegsmann.com

Julia Cameron
www.juliacameronlive.com

Narmada Akshat
www.innerlightheals.com

People for the Ethical Treatment of Animals (PETA)
501 Front St.
Norfolk, VA 23510
(757) 622-PETA (7382)

Pet Finder
www.petfinder.com

Silent Unity
www.unity.org / (757) 669-7729

Town of North Hempstead Animal Shelter
75 Marino Avenue
Port Washington, NY 11050-4207
(516) 944-8220

www.ingramcontent.com/pod-product-compliance
Lightning Source LLC
Chambersburg PA
CBHW051433280526
45785CB00003B/1266